Directory of Operating Grants

Second Edition

An Innovative Reference Directory
Pinpointing General Operating Grants
Available to Nonprofit Organizations

Research Grant Guides, Inc.
P.O. Box 1214
Loxahatchee, Florida 33470

© 1995 by Richard M. Eckstein

Richard M. Eckstein
Publisher/Editor

Andrew J. Grant, Ph.D.
Writer/Grant Consultant

Research and Administrative Staff:
Amy Bachmann
Claire L. Eckstein
Nancy Moore
Lorraine Moynihan
Debra Reese

Marketing Representative:
Cathy J. Tosner
President
CJ Marketing

No part of this book may be reproduced in a retrieval system or transmitted in any form or by any means, electronic, mechanical, photocopy, microfilming, recording or otherwise without written permission from Richard M. Eckstein.

Printed in the U.S.A.

ISSN 1071-6726
ISBN 0-945078-09-9

Table of Contents

    page

Preface 4

Foreword 5

Budget Strategies that Win Grants: Making Your Case with the Balance Sheet
    by Andrew J. Grant, Ph.D. 6

In Search of the Elusive Operating Grant
    by Andrew J. Grant, Ph.D. and Suzy D. Sonenberg, M.S.W. 16

Proposal Writing Basics by Andrew J. Grant, Ph.D. 21

Fund Raising's 20 Biggest and Most Costly Mistakes by Chris Petersen 24

Foundations 30

Appendices

    A—Bibliography of State and Local Foundation Directories 128

    B—The Foundation Center 135

    C—The Grantsmanship Center 142

Indices

    Alphabetical Index 143

    Subject Index 152

Preface

The second edition of the *Directory of Operating Grants* will assist fundraisers seeking grants for general operating funds. Operating grants can help nonprofit organizations underwrite salaries, rent, mortgage payments, utilities, office supplies, and additional overhead expenses.

The *Directory* profiles foundations that have awarded operating grants to nonprofit organizations. The following subject areas are profiled in the *Directory*: AIDS, animal welfare, community development, cultural organizations, disabled, education, elderly, environment, health organizations, higher education, hospitals, minorities, religious organizations, social welfare, women and youth organizations.

Funding sources may change their priorities and expenditure levels. Corporations and corporate foundations respond to the general economy and may curtail their grant-making programs until profits reach a satisfactory level. Don't be discouraged if your proposal is not funded on the first try.

To get started, use the *Directory* to research funding agencies supporting operating funds. Be careful to remember that many foundations and corporations award grants only in their own geographic area. Geographic restrictions and grant range are listed when available to our research staff. Next, send a brief letter to the funding agency and request a copy of their most recent grant guidelines, if they publish them. Guidelines issued by the funder should always be followed. Before writing a grant proposal, read the guidelines listed in *Proposal Writing Basics* beginning on page 21.

Several elements in a successful grant proposal include:

1) Uniqueness of proposal subject matter

2) A clear, well-written application

3) A realistic budget

4) Qualifications of the project Director

5) Issues of concern to the proposed sponsor

If the proposal warrants, there should be a table of contents to guide the reviewer. A timetable depicting your proposed progress also may be helpful. Try to present a readable, professional-looking proposal written in clear language that avoids jargon.

Foreword

Publication of the second edition of the *Directory of Operating Grants* responds to the increasing demand among not-for-profit organizations for assistance in identifying funding sources receptive to proposals for general operating support (sometimes called "unrestricted core support"). This directory will be of greatest assistance if the reader takes a moment to reflect on the meaning of general operating support.

For the purpose of contrast, we can assign grants to one of three broad categories. These are 1) project specific; 2) restricted core support; and 3) general operating. They can be distinguished as follows:

Project Grant: This type of grant supports activities related to a discrete, well-defined program conducted by an organization in addition to its routine business. A line-item budget, separate from the organization's overall budget, limits the use of funds to specific project activities. For example, funds for intiating a new service.

Restricted Core Support: This type of grant supports a specific line item or items in the core operating budget of an organization. The supported items often tend to be new additions (such as a new staff person and some related expenses) that require external support until they can be integrated into the organization's ongoing budget. Sometimes they are one-time expenses (such as the purchase of equipment or moving costs) that a funder agrees to underwrite.

General Operating Grant: This type of grant is not restricted to any discrete project or set of specified activities. It can be used to support the general ongoing operating expenses that support an organization's usual activities. Such unrestricted income helps an organization to carry out its goals without imposing the requirement to develop activities directly attributable to the grant.

Many funding organizations are reluctant to respond favorably to requests for operating support precisely because there will be no activities or results that can be identified with a specific grant. The ability to attribute specific projects and outcomes to their grants is a priority of most grant-making organizations.

In times of tight money, however, not-for-profit organizations often need income for survival. Fortunately, despite a general reluctance, there are funders willing to provide general support. This *Directory* will assist the seeker of operating grants in identifying those organizations.

Budget Strategies that Win Grants: Making Your Case with the Balance Sheet
by
Andrew J. Grant, Ph.D.

The budget is one of the most important parts of any proposal or project. Yet it is often regarded as an afterthought, tacked on after all other sections have been completed. Some find the budget a mystery, making the assumption that only an accountant or other financial professional is capable of constructing it. Budgets are neither complicated nor mysterious. They are, however, vital to the success of any grant proposal. Otherwise strong proposals can be undermined easily by lack of attention to budget detail. Implementing projects with poorly conceived budgets can lead to disaster running the program. This article is designed to serve as a guide to approaching and developing budgets. It is an orientation to the budgeting process for grant seekers eager to develop the most compelling proposals for their organizations. The following sections discuss how the budget serves as a planning tool. The article goes on to describe the elements that make up that process, using a project oriented proposal as an example. Using this as a foundation, we will explore budgeting issues as they relate to proposals for operating grants.

More Than Just Numbers

Columns of numbers arranged in categories and displayed on one or more pages are only representations of the budget. Budgeting is a process through which an idea evolves into a plan of operation. It certainly results in a display of numbers, but the primary function of the budget is to serve as the central planning mechanism for any project or proposal. True for any type of proposal, recognition of the vital role played by the budget process is especially important for operating grants.

Every proposal starts out with an idea. The idea usually is based on some need perceived among the clients of a nonprofit organization. Let's take increasing demand for child care services as an example. Sensing the urgency of this need, a nonprofit community oriented organization decides to seek funding to organize and operate a child care center and hires a consultant to help write the proposal.

The consultant listens to the staff of the organization describe the community in terms of demographics and geography as they relate to the proposed project. The staff have done a lot of homework, including research on job patterns, increase in the number of

---

Andrew J. Grant, Ph.D. is Director of Grants at Baruch College/CUNY. He also teaches a graduate course on grants administration at Hofstra University, Hempstead, New York. Dr. Grant has been involved with sponsored project administration for twenty years.

Dr. Grant has written grant proposals that were successfully funded from corporations, foundations and government agencies. He conducts workshops and publishes articles on varied topics in fund-raising. He received his Ph.D. in Public Administration from New York University. His e-mail address is agrbb@cunyvm.cuny.edu. Dr. Grant and his wife Mindy are principals in the consulting firm Grant Services Corp.

families in which both parents work, number of latchkey children and availability of child care services in the area. They feel they have already conducted a substantial amount of planning and expect their consultant to take the information, begin researching sources of support and start writing the proposal.

The consultant asks only one question, the answer to which will make clear whether the nonprofit has indeed done the necessary planning to start the grant seeking process. "How much will it cost?" The confused look among the staff tells the consultant that the organization has only an idea which still must be worked into an effective project plan. The executive director of the organization notes that although the project has been planned out, little thought has been given to the details of a budget. Another staff member asks, "How much can we get?" Another adds, "It will probably be several million dollars." To which someone else answers, "It couldn't possibly be that much."

Budgeting Equals Planning

Our consultant in the example above will take the organization through a project planning process using the budget as the central point of focus. The question, "How much will it cost?", includes three other questions. These are:

"What do we want to do?"
"What resources do we need to accomplish it?"
"How much will each resource cost?"

These questions form the central core of any project or proposal plan. In the example, our hypothetical organization identified a need in the community and determined that a child care program would be an effective means toward meeting that need. They had gathered information to justify the statement of need and then assumed they were ready to begin the proposal writing process. In fact, they had answered only the first of the three questions posed above.

Unfortunately, many grant seekers proceed exactly the same way, postponing consideration of cost factors until the end of the process. Proposals constructed this way often reflect a lack of planning that causes them to fail in funding competition.

A better strategy begins by determining the resources needed to conduct the project. It's wise to start with a "best case" approach. At first, the project should be envisioned as though total cost is not a restriction. The process progresses through a series of steps leading to a well defined proposal supported by a realistic budget.

Step 1 - Consider All Possible Options

The process begins with a discussion of available options for conducting the project. In our child care example, the group responsible for planning would consider issues related to facilities, staff, schedules, fees, recruitment, programming and operations. Choices must be made about each set of issues. For example, where will the facility be housed? Who will staff it? What will be its hours of operation? What type of fee structure will be implemented?

Stating each major issue at the top of a page or column and listing all the options under it is an effective way to visualize the choices. Computer word processing or spreadsheet programs facilitate the process, but a piece of paper works well if no computer is available. Proceeding with our example, there would be a page or column with the heading "Facilities". All possible alternatives would be listed. They might include the following:

- construct a new facility;
- purchase an existing facility;
- purchase and modify an existing facility;
- lease an existing facility;
- lease and modify an existing facility;
- renovate space owned by the organization;
- obtain donated space;
- collaborate with another organization that already operates a child care program.

Identifying a comprehensive list of possibilities is an important part of the process at this stage. It may require one or more group sessions in which the planners are open to listing any idea, no matter how complicated, feasible or expensive it may seem. The task is to develop as long a list of options as possible.

Step 2 - Predict And Evaluate The Outcomes Of Each Option

Each option listed in Step 1 now becomes the heading of its own page or double column. Step 2 is the most complicated and time consuming. Each alternative course of action must be evaluated in terms of positive and negative consequences. Constructing a new facility, for example, has the advantage of providing space custom designed for the organization's program. It has the disadvantages of being an expensive and lengthy process. It also requires the availability of a building lot. If the organization already owns suitable property, this option holds greater promise than if land acquisition is an additional factor.

Purchasing an existing facility may be less expensive and provide space with as much usefulness as custom designed construction. How much difference would there be in cost? Are any facilities available? How much modification would be required? Obviously, more research is needed before these questions can be answered. Our planners may find out that even though construction will be more expensive, the resulting structure will be so much better that it will be worth the additional cost, time and effort toward securing funds. Or they may determine just the opposite.

The point is that these alternatives cannot be evaluated adequately without the extensive planning described here. The more complicated the project or program, the more complicated will be the planning process.

Step 3 - Select The Best Option

When all the options included under all the planning issues have been evaluated, the planners can proceed to selecting the best. Remember that at this point, we haven't calculated specific costs. We have explored the options only in terms of their effectiveness in developing a project that will satisfy the need for child care services in the community to the maximum extent possible. We have a blueprint of a "best case" project.

Step 4 - How Much Will It Cost?

Each of the options we select has fiscal implications. In this step our planners will determine the cost of each component of the program. The cost of facilities, salaries and benefits, materials, furniture and fixtures and other items considered in Steps 1, 2 and 3 must be determined. This may require additional research. We must also predict program income, if any. Each of the items, grouped in categories would be listed in a budget format with the item on the left side of the page and the cost on the right. The sum of costs - "the bottom line" - is the total cost of the project.

Our best case project budget may be well within the organizational ability to raise necessary funds; it may be far beyond that ability or it may be somewhere between the two. At this point, the project planners may be forced to make adjustments. They will go back to Stage 2 and substitute less expensive options if the total project exceeds feasible limits, or they may expand the project plan if they've been too conservative.

Having built a best case budget, they have equipped themselves with the information necessary to make the most rational choices for proceeding with the fund raising strategies. Whether they scale back the project, expand it or abandon it altogether, the planners of our fictional nonprofit organization know that the project developed through the budgeting/planning process will meet the needs of their clients and will be feasible and cost effective. Their proposal will include a description of the planning process, specifying alternatives considered and rejected to arrive at the final proposed components. That proposal will be much more competitive than one based on less comprehensive planning.

Budget Issues For Operating Grants

The process described above is known as the Classical or Rational model of decision making. As noted, it can be used in many settings. It helps structure a complex project by identifying issues and presenting alternative courses of action for consideration. As shown, it is an excellent mechanism for both program and budget planning. It is the same process we use daily, consciously or unconsciously, in making decisions from what movie to see or rent to which car to buy or lease. The more complicated the decision, the more we make a conscious effort to plan for the outcome.

The model can be especially helpful in structuring proposals for operating grants even though such proposals *do not* focus on one specific project. A review of the elements of an operating grant proposal will help show how this model can strengthen an organization's appeal for operating funds.

How We Ask For Operating Funds

When an organization applies for operating funds, it seeks to supplement its regular sources of income. These additional funds are sought to help maintain services or programs already being provided by that organization. In some cases, operating grants are needed to expand existing services. A copy of my previous article, "In Search of the Elusive Operating Grant", is reprinted in this issue of the Directory. It describes the major differences between project and operating grants as well as similarities and differences in the strategies used in proposals for these two grant types. It also details why many funding sources seem reluctant to support operations.

In writing proposals for operating grants, applicants typically will describe the needs filled by their organizations, characterize the clients and communities they serve and discuss the fiscal realities of trying to satisfy the demands for increased services with shrinking income streams. They will research foundations and other sources listing operating grants among their priorities and ask for an amount somewhere within the grant range of those sponsors. The typical operating grant proposal does not have a central project focus and devotes much less attention to budget detail or to a justification of the dollar amount it specifies in the proposal. The typical operating grant proposal is also likely to fail.

Inadequate Planning Often Results In The Need For Operating Funds

The reluctance to support operating grants among many sponsors stems from the perception that many such grants serve only to perpetuate inefficient management practices. Well managed organizations, the argument goes, would not be in need of additional or emergency operating funds if their directors and managers planned effectively for fiscal fluctuations. Promoting dependency among grantee organizations is another concern of some sponsors. If the grant is made, what measures will be taken to ensure that the nonprofit organization will regain and maintain self-sufficiency? Will the sponsor be asked for additional operating grants in successive years? If so, for how long?

In many cases, these concerns are well founded. Nonprofit organizations can get into trouble if they fail to predict reduction or total elimination of some income sources or increased demand for services. Too often, proposals for operating funds are appeals for emergency funding needed to withstand a fiscal crisis. Such crisis situations often arise because fiscal managers engage in the common practice of incremental budgeting. Typically, organizational officials develop budgets for a new year simply by increasing each budget category from the previous year by a percentage keyed to the rate of inflation. Thus, the original budget increases by small "increments" year after year.

Incrementalism generally works well, especially in stable times. It is practiced by budget developers in for-profit and government organizations as well as by those in nonprofit organizations. Managers will get into trouble, however, if they fail to predict and respond to changes in income streams or in service demands and continue to base budgets on those of previous years. Such lack of active planning can result in cash shortfalls if unpredicted changes occur. Sponsors are wary when they review operating grant proposals that communicate needs based on crises resulting from inadequate planning.

Budget Strategies For Operating Grant Proposals

Requests for operating funds that are in fact attempts to survive from one fiscal crisis to the next stand little chance of being successful. If the organization does secure the necessary funding, it will be wise to use the time provided by the grant to review and change its planning and budgeting practices. It certainly stands little prospect of continuing to obtain emergency funding from year to year.

It is important to note at this point that good proposals for operating grants are reflections of good planning. No amount of proposal writing skill can compensate for inadequate management and budget practices. The following discussion of the budget's role in securing operating grants is based on the understanding that organizational leaders make a commitment to analyze policies and practices and revise any found to be detrimental to fiscal stability. Sponsors expect that organizations in the position of needing operating funds have reviewed the reason or reasons leading to the appeal for such funding. Proposals will be competitive only if they communicate an understanding of the applicant's fiscal profile and history. Use of the Classical/Rational model will not only make for better proposals, but will also strengthen the organization itself.

Most foundations request applicants to submit a copy of the most recent audited financial report as part of the proposal package. In more than a few cases, the information contained in that report can make the difference between funding and rejection. The audited financial report or statement is a copy of the organization's budget for the fiscal year most recently completed. It is prepared and certified by an accounting firm retained by the organization. Foundations request it because it provides a picture of the applicant's fiscal health and priorities. Many applicants include it with the proposal simply because the sponsor requested it. In an operating grant proposal, it is a mistake to attach the financial report without making reference to it. In fact, a well structured proposal can use the financial report as the central focus of the appeal.

As noted in the foreword, there is a difference between general operating funds and restricted core support. In either case, referencing the request to the audited financial report will make the proposal clearer and stronger. The applicant should describe the need for support in terms of its overall operating budget, as depicted in the financial statement. It should be open and honest about the need and how it came about. If the reason is lack of planning, the proposal should state that. The proposal must include a description of the steps being taken to correct previously inadequate planning practices. It must also include a plan describing how the requested grant will help the organization regain self sufficiency.

Here's where the rational planning model comes in. The operating grant proposal would describe the current need and discuss how the organization has restructured its planning to ensure future fiscal health. Such a proposal might be structured with the following components. I've posed these as questions in the interest of clarity. Any style that deals with these issues is appropriate.

How Did The Current Situation Arise?

This is another way of asking why the grant is being requested. The writer should make reference to areas of the financial report that are applicable. For example, the financial statement might show that demand for and income from a particular service declined, but that the resources devoted to that service were maintained too long. Perhaps the staffing level of the entire organization is too rich. Whatever the case, reference to the financial report will support the argument. It describes how the operating budget was derived and distributed. The proposal narrative should point out areas of inefficiency and describe why they came about.

If the request is for restricted core support, the argument might be that demand for a service increased dramatically. This might have been for demographic reasons - an influx of immigration to the area. Perhaps the reasons were based in economics - a sudden increase in unemployment may have occurred. The proposal should discuss these factors and point out that the budget, as shown in the financial report, cannot support any new positions. Whatever the specific case, the point is that the discussion in the proposal should be linked to the previous operating budget.

What Have We Done To Correct The Situation?

This section of the proposal cannot be written until the organizational leadership performs the analysis and revision of policy and procedures discussed earlier. Once that's been done, the proposal can proceed to describe what should be a rational planning process applied to the organization's total operations and budget. The organization is in trouble. The foundation wants assurance that it will be asked only to help get that organization on the road to eliminating the need for operating funds.

The steps in this process parallel the four steps described earlier in the discussion of how the budget planning for a new community health facility took place. The organization should review its mission, goals and activities. Are they all appropriate? Where can cuts be made? What services must be retained? What is the plan to implement any changes? This process is often termed "zero-based" planning or budgeting. It looks at an activity as though there were no history. It is the opposite of incremental planning. In the process we look at the needs of the clients and design services to meet them. We consider the alternatives and their outcomes and determine the cost of the most appropriate alternatives. This can be an agonizing process of organizational soul searching, but a necessary one if survival is at stake. It is nothing short of evaluating everything the organization does and then restructuring its activities where necessary.

Where Does The Operating Grant Fit In?

This is critical to the proposal. It contrasts the previous and future organizational budgets and describes how the grant of operating funds will help meet the new goals the organization has set in response to the planning it conducted. The discussion should include a time schedule. Perhaps a one time grant will be sufficient. Perhaps the organization will need support over a number of years, but in diminishing quantities. There should be a discussion of income sources and their relationship to the restructured operating budget as well as to those activities that have been dropped, added or sustained. If the proposal is for a new service, it should describe the income that service will provide. This discussion helps the foundation see that the organization has done a great deal of planning aimed at repositioning itself. It provides assurance that the foundation will not be placed in the role of savior, but that its grant is part of a larger reorganization plan.

A Difficult Process

This is a difficult process. Organizational managers and trustees obviously will need courage and honesty to submit proposals structured as described above. The process of reorganization and reevaluation can be stressful. The first step in securing operating grants, however, is to recognize the conditions contributory to the organization's need for an operating grant. Analyzing an organizational mission can be revitalizing. If successful, the organization will become stronger and better serve the needs of its clients. If its proposals reflect an orderly and honest self study and evaluation, they will earn the respect and support of potential sponsors.

SAMPLE PROPOSAL BUDGET SUMMARY FOR A PROJECT

		AMOUNT
I.	SALARIES AND WAGES	$ 228,081
II.	FRINGE BENEFITS	45,616
III.	PERMANENT EQUIPMENT	24,315
IV.	SUPPLIES	33,445
V.	TRAVEL	830
VI.	CONSULTANT FEES	970
VII.	COMPUTER COSTS	6,500
VIII.	SERVICES	4,150
IX.	RENOVATION	12,500
X.	INDIRECT COSTS	136,849
TOTAL PROJECT COSTS		**$493,256**

SAMPLE PROPOSAL BUDGET FOR A PROJECT

	AMOUNT
I. SALARIES AND WAGES	
A. Senior Personnel	
1. Project Director/Medical Director 100% x $75,000	$ 75,000
2. Mary Best, RN, Assistant Director 20% x $50,000	10,000
Subtotal Senior Personnel Salaries	**85,000**
B. Senior Professionals	
1. Robert Johnson, Gerontologist 100% x $50,000	50,000
2. John Scofield, Sr. Staff Associate 50% x $35,000	17,500
3. To Be Determined, Systems Manager 100% x $27,500	27,500
Subtotal Senior Professional Salaries	**95,000**
C. Other Personnel	
1. Respite Care Assistants	
a. John Lincoln 100% x $12,000	12,000
b. Michelle Smith 50% x $12,000	6,000
c. To Be Determined 100% x $12,000	12,000
2. Technical Support	
a. Elizabeth Bent, Electronics Technician 50% x $20,000	10,000
3. Administrative/Clerical Support	
a. Patricia Clark, Administrative Asst. 20% x $26,250	5,250
b. Michael Benson, Clerk Typist 15% x $18,870	2,831
Subtotal Other Personnel	**48,081**
Total Salaries And Wages	**$228,081**

	AMOUNT

II. FRINGE BENEFITS
    A. Senior Personnel (20% x $180,000) .... $ 36,000
    B. Other Personnel (20% x $48,080) 9,616
Total Fringe Benefits $45,616

III. PERMANENT EQUIPMENT
    A. Life Support Equipment 24,315
Total Permanent Equipment $24,315

IV. SUPPLIES
    A. Medical 22,995
    B. Office 6,750
    C. Computer 3,700
Total Supplies $33,445

V. TRAVEL
    A. Domestic
        1. AMA Convention in Albuquerque, NM
            a. Airfare: round-trip 400
            b. Hotel: 3 nights @ $50/night 150
            c. Subsistence: 3 days @ $35/day 105
            d. Car rental: 3 days @ $45/day 135
            e. Taxis (NYC) 40
Total Travel $830

VI. CONSULTANT FEES
    A. Dr. F. Wargarten, Univ. of Calif., San Diego
        2 days @ $285/day 570
    B. Dr. O. Wells, Univ. of Washington: 2 days @ $200/day 400
Total Consultant Fees $970

VII. COMPUTER COSTS
    A. Scanner 2,500
    B. Apple MacIntosh Quadra 800 2,500
    C. Medical Information Systems (AcIS)
        100 hours @ $15/hour 1,500
Total Computer Costs $6,500

	AMOUNT
VIII. SERVICES	
A. Maintenance Agreements	
1. Apple Computer	$ 1,200
2. IBM Personal Computer	200
3. Photocopier	2,000
B. Photocopying	750
Total Services	**$4,150**
IX. RENOVATION	
A. Partition Installation	10,000
B. Rewiring for installation of specialized equipment	2,500
Total Renovation	**$12,500**
TOTAL DIRECT COSTS	**$356,407**
X. INDIRECT COSTS	
A. Overhead: 60% of salaries and wages	136,849
Total Indirect Costs	**$136,849**
TOTAL PROJECT COSTS	**$493,256**

In Search of the Elusive Operating Grant
by
Andrew J. Grant, Ph.D.
and Suzy D. Sonenberg, M.S.W.

The concept of philanthropic support applied to general operating budgets of non-profit organizations continues to generate controversy. The debate is neither new nor limited to any grant-making sector. There is also a lack of consensus regarding a precise definition of operating grants. Our foreword to this edition of the *Directory of Operating Grants* describes how we characterize this type of grant.

Government agencies, foundations and corporations traditionally have been reluctant to grant funds for day-to-day operations. Yet, unrestricted grants are considered essential by many non-profit organizations. Their continuing ability to provide services and, in some cases, their survival may depend on such support.

The Appeal Of Project Grants

The tendency among funding agencies or donors to favor the special project grant originates from several factors. The project grant is visible and identifiable with the funding source. It is made for a limited time period to accomplish a specific goal or goals. It can be evaluated to determine how well the goals were realized.

Project grants are powerful tools for grant-makers. Government agencies can utilize them to implement competitive grant programs to accomplish priorities when available allocations are insufficient to fund all eligible applicants. The competitive process is favored also for its ability to generate new and compelling ideas from creative thinkers. Rigorous standards and fierce competition have advanced the national scientific agenda through the process of applying for grants.

Foundations generally believe that making operating grants detracts from the basic purpose of foundation funding, which is to support new ideas and help start new programs that otherwise would not be implemented. A dramatic example is that of the Ford Foundation and its involvement in New York City public school decentralization between 1967 and 1970. A grant from Ford helped support a small number of demonstration districts within the school system in order to try out the concept of administration of education in a community based setting. The project became part of one of the most contentious periods in New York City school politics and eventually led to the decentralization of the system. Ford was able to make an impact on a controversial issue and also limit its involvement to a short time period with a grant modest in size in comparison to the total operating budget of the school system.

The ability to evaluate the outcome of project grants also contributes to the appeal of this type of funding. The concept of accountability inevitably leads to the question, "How effective were the activities supported by this grant?". Special projects are conducted in addition to the regular activities of an agency; financial and program data must be maintained and reported separately from the other business of the organization. The ease of determining how the project worked permits the funder to evaluate the original decision to make the grant and also helps determine whether additional funding is warranted.

Project grants have helped recipient organizations meet the needs of their constituencies. Many grantee organizations have generated support for programs that enhanced their services. Countless grant-initiated projects eventually became incorporated into the routine services provided by non-profit organizations. A few matured into national institutions. Not many people realize that Sesame Street was started with a small grant to try out the idea that television could be used as an educational tool.

The Need For Operating Funds

Non-profit organizations, despite the positive outcomes of project grant funding, are faced with receding income streams. Many argue that initiating new projects for which grants must be sought is a luxury they can no longer afford. Their needs are basic and pressing as they struggle to deliver services to their constituencies, and they are looking to the grant-making community to support those basic operations.

The community of non-profit organizations is feeling the impact of diminishing financial support. Periods of economic downturn reduce the value of endowments, where they exist, and make investment portfolios less reliable sources of income. All sectors of the economy are affected similarly, resulting in reduced capacity for foundations and corporations to respond to increased requests. Government programs also cut back during hard times.

As service providers, the non-profits feel the repercussions of the recession in increased demand for services. Non-profit agencies perform the function of filling in gaps found in the mosaic of government social service, health, education and advocacy programs. If non-profit agencies did not exist, their services would need to be provided by government agencies at taxpayer expense or would not be available at all.

Non-profit administrators argue that the traditional model of funding must change to accommodate economic conditions. That model describes a system in which project grant funding provides support to start programs with seed money. If these programs prove successful, they must be continued through government reimbursement or become self-sustaining. As noted above, this project grant model has been used to generate new ideas and programs that promote the mission of the not-for-profit service sector.

The rationale for moving away from this model is that funding is so scarce it is all too frequently impossible to continue programs even if they show promise during the stage of initiation. Administrators argue, furthermore, that developing new program ideas and seeking project grants to implement them detracts energy from providing basic services to increasingly needy clients.

Moving toward acceptance of making operating fund grants on a broader scale will require a fundamental change in the way funding organizations see their role. There may be some movement in that direction, but it is unrealistic to expect a wholesale shift from project to operating grants, even in the short run. The philosophical debate will continue as change evolves.

What Expectations Are Realistic?

It is possible to obtain grants for operations within the context of the current environment. Realistic expectations and the same intensive research needed to identify any type of grant are two basic resources necessary to secure operating funds. To be avoided in any approach for such support is the attitude, born of frustration, that the grant-making community should be changing its policies and practices. That argument belongs on an editorial page or letter to the editor, not in a proposal. Increased need and reduced funding in themselves will not generate grants for operations.

Funding agencies listing operating support among their priorities are far fewer than those willing to grant funds for more restricted activities. Research is the all important first step. The research process, however, will be more intense and will involve a few extra steps beyond the process followed to identify support for project grants.

The first and obvious step is to identify all funders in the applicant's geographic area, as well as foundations with a national focus, that support activities related to the organizational mission and that list operating funds among their priorities. Such a search is likely to yield only a few prospects simply because the universe of grantors who support operations is so small. In a routine search, the prospects so identified would form the basis for further research and proposal submission. For an operating fund grant an additional step is necessary.

The applicant should also compile a list of all sources in the geographic area and those funding nationally that support activities related to the applicant's organizational mission and who don't identify operating grants as a possibility, but don't exclude them either. Work with this second list may provide viable sources that otherwise would not have been identified. The most important part of the process is how the proposal presents the request.

What To Say And Not Say In The Proposal

The elements of a proposal for operating support are no different from those found in any other good proposal. The key is to appeal to the funder in terms of a shared agenda. The research discussed above will have identified those sources whose agenda is consistent with that of the applicant organization. The focus of the proposal should be on the mission and important work of the organization, not on the organizational need for operating support.

A useful analogy is to think of the proposal as a prospectus for a stock offering. How many of us would rush to buy stock if a broker called to advise that unless we invest, the company will go out of business? Who would race to write a check to help a company whose finances are so bad it can't continue to produce its product or service unless it gets an infusion of cash, over many years to keep it from going bankrupt?

Few of us would be inclined to invest our money. Yet, this is precisely the tone of many proposals seeking operational support for non-profit organizations. Grant-making organizations are less likely to invest in non-profit grant applicants who appear to be bad risks. Grants go to organizations that are likely to be successful in carrying out activities advancing the concerns shared with the potential funder. Remembering the following points will help keep the proposal focused on those concerns.

- When applying to funders who list operating grants among their priorities, the proposal should present the needs to be addressed, as well as the nature of the service provided, describe the applicant organization and request a dollar amount consistent with the giving history of the foundation, corporation or individual. Again, such information is gained as the result of intense, comprehensive research.

- For funders who do not specifically exclude operating grants, but don't list them as a priority, the proposal needs to make a strong case for the need for service provided by the organization and then provide a compelling rationale for operating support. Pleading poverty works no better in this context than it would in the case of our fictitious stock offering. The proposal writer has the difficult, but not impossible, job of persuading the potential grantor to deviate from its routine and comfortable practices.

- When there is a client population receiving services, a thorough description of that population is critical to this approach. The proposal should speak in terms of unique or critical services to ignored, neglected or isolated populations that are of interest to the prospective funder. It should describe the applicant agency in terms of experience, reliability, knowledge about the service and client group. The proposal needs to be written from a position of strength.

- The most difficult part of writing is the transition from that description of a strong organization to the need for operating funds. The writer must avoid damaging inconsistencies that erode the reader's impression of a strong organization. The proposal should not convey the message that the applicant organization is incapable of providing service because of cuts in income.

- The strongest approach is to detail the services offered to the constituency and identify how such activities have been funded. A discussion of which income streams have been eliminated or curtailed should follow. The next step is to discuss the impact of such cuts on the service. This approach keeps the focus on the needs of the client and the consequences of funding limitations.

- The request for a dollar amount should be specific and linked to the expected duration such funding will be needed. The more limited and restricted the request, the greater the chance it will be funded. For example, an appeal for short term, emergency funding necessary until another income source can be put in place will have a better chance than a request for a long term, non-specific grant. Grant requests restricted to specific activities of the agency will also fare better than an amorphous appeal for general operating funds.

- It is important to provide the grantor a limited time horizon. The proposal should give the funder a way out by deflecting the impression that long term assistance is required. The strongest case would be from an applicant who could anticipate or plan for replacement funding over the long term. References to funding bills in the state or federal legislatures for the services provided by the agency give the assurance that other help may be on the way and that the applicant is aware of future funding options.

- Finally, it is also vital to document the planning process to be followed in replacing diminishing funds. Such items in the proposal provide the assurance and comfort to the grantor that the applicant has done its homework in exhausting all possible avenues of support. The foundation or corporation considering the request thereby feels it can make a contribution without being the sole source of support for the applicant.

Not all applicants will be able to make their case in such detailed and comprehensive terms. Those who can follow this outline, however, will have the greatest potential for succeeding in this difficult arena.

Proposal Writing Basics
by
Andrew J. Grant, Ph.D.

Despite the availability of excellent references on the subject, proposal writing still seems an elusive art. Many of my colleagues working in foundations, corporations and government agencies despair at the poor quality of proposals they receive.

Proposals that fail to communicate effectively jeopardize the support that might be granted to an otherwise excellent project. Competition for funds is fierce. Many worthwhile projects must be declined because so many organizations pursue the limited dollars available. Poorly written proposals simply make it easy for the funder to reject the request; there are too many good ones to consider. For the pressured funder, it is impractical to spend time trying to make sense of unclear proposals.

I will add my voice to those who have written about this subject. Perhaps the best place to begin is with some fundamental, axiomatic observations about the process.

Some Truths That Should Be Self-Evident

• Research, not writing, is the first step. Funders have specific interests. These must be researched. Proposals should be submitted only to those sources that have articulated a priority in the type of project to be undertaken by the applicant. To do otherwise is like going shopping for groceries in a hardware store. The response can only be, "You're in the wrong place."

• Proposal writing requires a good writer. Communicating in clear, precise English assumes talent that not everyone possesses. Sometimes a proposal writer is in the wrong job. I've seen this more than occasionally in the training seminars I conduct. Although proposal writing is an excellent way to enter the fund-raising profession, it's not for everyone. Skills must be assessed accurately by the employer and job seeker. Writing is only one specialty required in fund-raising. People uncomfortable with writing can find many other rewarding career paths in professional fund-raising.

• Follow directions. Many funders provide specific instructions on what they want in a submission. If such directions exist, they should be adhered to without deviation. Frequently, however, there are no specific guidelines. For such cases the following outline provides a model of what should be contained in a proposal. The model is basic and flexible enough to accommodate different writing styles.

Starting: The Most Difficult Part

Questions that are asked frequently are, "How should the proposal begin?" and "What is the best way to introduce the subject?" The opening paragraph is of vital importance. It must set the stage and interest the reader enough to make him or her want to know more. All this in two or three sentences.

A most effective way to do this is to begin with a general or global statement of the problem to be addressed. Let's use the example of a project to provide neighborhood transportation for people with disabilities.

For example:
"The absence of accessible transportation constitutes a serious obstacle to people with disabilities in performing the routine tasks of everyday life."

This opening sentence would be followed by two or three other short statements. Their purpose is to focus the general issue to be addressed in the context of the local environment. These statements serve the purpose of describing how this issue manifests itself in the particular situation that is the subject of the proposal. The entire introduction should occupy no more than a half page of a three-page letter or a full page of a five-page formal proposal. Included might be some statistics descriptive of the severity of the problem and the population to be served.

Who Are You? Dealing From Strength

The second paragraph or section should describe the agency or organization proposing to conduct the project. The most important thing to remember here is not to assume any knowledge on the part of the reader. It is easy to become too familiar with an issue or organization. The effect on the proposal when this happens is an inadequate description. That's fatal to the case. The prospective funder must have a clear idea of precisely who the applicant is.

A good way to handle this section is to write several descriptions of the organization in advance. They should be of varying length. Taking time to do this pays off in descriptions that present the agency in its most favorable light.

That brings up another vital consideration. The proposing agency must convince the funder that it is the best choice to conduct a project dealing with the subject issue. Using our example of a transportation program, the description should touch upon the following items:

- knowledge of the client population
- knowledge of the geographic area to be served
- experience in providing the service proposed
- familiarity with the issue
- qualifications of the staff
- acceptance in the community

If an agency cannot present a compelling capability statement without exaggerating, it needs to revaluate its reasons for seeking funds for the project. Funders strive to invest in organizations that have the ability to put grants to maximum use. This description of capabilities, therefore, is probably the most important information to be covered in a proposal.

How Much Will It Cost?

This is no place to be bashful. The amount of money requested should be indicated as early as possible in the proposal. Ideally it should be included in the first paragraph. The dollar request says a lot about the project. It establishes limits. It tells the funder the extent of its participation. It says something about cost effectiveness. Finally, if the request is realistic, not too high or low for the funder to whom it's directed, it tells that funder the applicant has done his or her homework.

What Will Be Different?

Until now we've been carefully setting the stage. We've prepared the reader to be interested in the project, which now must be described. What are the goals? How will it work? Who will benefit? Who will do the work? What will have been accomplished?

In order for the description to be compelling, the project must have been well thought out. The heart of a good proposal is a good project. When the program has been well planned, this part of the proposal is easy to write. If that's not the case, the project planning must be reexamined. Often, project weaknesses become exposed in the act of attempting a written description that simply won't flow.

Other Considerations

Because writing styles are so individual, proposals will vary even if they are based on a common model. In all cases, the project itself will determine what is appropriate to include and omit. For example, a statement regarding how the agency will measure success is important. The formality and complexity of the evaluation design, however, will vary greatly.

Many funders like to know whose company they are keeping. It's often useful to indicate what other sources of funding there are.

Finally, each organization has ancillary materials that can be appended to a proposal. A certificate of nonprofit status and an audited financial statement are standards. Other attachments should be included only if they make a contribution to the case.

In closing, it bears noting that proposal writing takes practice. It is a skill that requires development. This model provides a guide to the structure of a proposal. Substance and style are very much a function of the individual writer.

Fund Raising's 20 Biggest and Most Costly Mistakes
Don't You Make Them
by
Chris Petersen

Call them what you will - gaffes, blunders, oversights, or errors - mistakes creep into everyone's professional life. But in fund raising - unlike other fields - where thousands if not millions of dollars are often on the table, mistakes can be especially hazardous.

Who hasn't forfeited a significant gift, or received but a token one; due to some serious miscalculation? While there may be hundreds of them, 20 potentially costly fund raising mistakes stand out. They can't really be ranked, since circumstances alter their impact. But they can be outlined, as I've done below, in an effort to ward you away from them.

Thinking your organization will attract support simply because it's a good cause.

Just because you have a good cause - one of thousands, really - doesn't mean money will wend its way to you. Organizations must attract support the old fashioned way - earn it.

Giving away money is something we all do reluctantly, and it's hardly an instinctive act. Nonetheless, people will support you if you present them with a challenging project that is consistent with their interests. To succeed, you must explain exactly why you seek the funding, why your project is compelling, who will benefit, and why the money is needed now. In other words, your needs - presented as opportunities - must be specific, people-oriented, and have a sense of urgency.

Keep in mind, always, that people give in order to get. They don't simply want to give away their money, they want to feel they're investing it and getting something in return.

Thinking that others can raise the money for you.

Successful fund raising abides by the "rock in the pond" principle. That is, you can't expect others to contribute until those closest to the center of your organization do so. The farther from the center, the weaker the interest. In short, solicitation starts with your inner "family" - most notably the board. Only when these individuals have made proportionately generous contributions, do you reach out to your external constituency.

Why this principle? Because it only makes sense that if a board approves a program involving significant outlays, with the understanding that money has to be raised, then these same trustees must commit themselves to giving and getting. If your governing body won't do so, who will?

The article appeared in the March/April 1994 issue of Contributions magazine and is reprinted with permission from the publisher. To subscribe, write Contributions, 634 Commonwealth Avenue, Suite 201, Newton Centre, MA 02159. $24 per year.

Believing that because people are wealthy they will contribute to you.

Simply because someone is wealthy, or thought to be wealthy, is no reason to assume that he or she will want to give to your project. This is the thinking of neophytes.

People make gifts, substantial gifts that is, only after you've reached out, informed them of your work, *and* meaningfully involved them in your organization. It is then that the prospective donor understands your goals, recognizes their importance, and welcomes the opportunity to have an impact. Solicitation rightfully becomes the final step in the fund raising process, not the first one.

Thinking you can whisk wealthy prospects in at the last minute.

Individuals, if they are to be committed to your organization, must have the opportunity to be involved in your work - and not at the 11th hour.

Intensively courting prospects just prior to your fund raising drive is an insulting ploy, and most are smart enough to know what you're up to. Much more advisable is to continuously involve prospects, for just as the best trustees are those who are meaningfully involved, the best contributors - and best solicitors too - are involved in your drive from conception to victory. Dollars, as Jerold Panas notes, follow commitment. And commitment follows involvement.

Failing to research and evaluate prospects.

Rarely do meaningful gifts come from strangers. Most major donors are either associated with an organization or have logical reasons to give. It is the role of prospect research to reveal these logical reasons by focusing on three elements: linkage, ability, and interest.

Is there any link between the prospective donor and your organization? If so, then this link - and it must be legitimate - makes an appointment with the prospect possible. Next is the person's ability to give. Does the prospect have enough discretionary income to justify your soliciting him or her for a major gift? Research will tell you the answer. Finally, what is the prospect's interest in your organization? If he or she has little interest or limited knowledge about you, then you will likely receive a small gift if any at all.

Failing to ask.

Very often, when campaigns fail, it's not because people didn't give, it's because they weren't asked. In fund raising, asking is the name of the game. The problem is, only for the rarest person is asking for a gift easy. For most of us, the discomfort is so strong we'll invent 100 excuses to procrastinate.

Despite any training, despite any inspirational send-off, asking will always be the biggest challenge. What can temper the fear to some degree is keeping in mind that prospects, who are usually more sensitive than we expect, respond favorably to solicitors who are dedicated and genuinely enthusiastic about the cause they represent.

Thinking that publicity or written materials will raise money.

Publicity, despite our best wishes, doesn't raise money. If you have solicitors and prospects, a strong case, and a campaign plan, you won't need any publicity. Those who do insist on a big splash are, more often than not, people who don't want to face the rigors of a campaign. When the publicity push fails to create a stir, they use it as an excuse for not working.

As for campaign materials, most serious donors see them as non-essential. They much prefer a persuasive verbal presentation, underscored by simple documentation. So long as you treat your press releases, brochures, drawings, or photographs as aids and not as solicitation devices, they will be useful but they will never take the place of direct asking.

Failing to recruit the right trustees.

Of all the groups important to an organization, none is more vital than the board of directors. There are exceptions, to be sure, but in 99 out of 100 cases an organization which consistently attracts the funding it needs has a board that accepts fund raising as a major responsibility, despite any other governing duties. Put another way, an organization's ability to raise money is almost always in direct proportion to the quality and dedication of its leadership. As Hank Rosso, founder of the Fund Raising School puts it, "People who have the fire of leadership burning within their souls, and who have that deep commitment to the organization's mission, will drive any program through to success."

Believing you can raise money by the multiplication table.

People new to fund raising often get it in their heads that all you have to do is divide your goal by the number of likely donors, then ask everyone to give an equal amount. But you can't raise money adequately by the multiplication table - trying, for instance, to get 1,000 persons to give $1,000. There are several inherent problems here. First, not everyone will give (which throws a wrench into the whole approach). Second, we all tend to give in relation to others. If someone, five times wealthier than you, pledges $1,000, are you likely to feel a $1,000 pledge from you is fair? Third, seeking $1,000 from each donor in effect sets a ceiling on what an unusually generous person might wish to pledge.

Failing to have deadlines.

By nature most of us are procrastinators, and whenever we have plenty of time, well, we seldom get it done. For many if not most volunteers, the thought of asking someone for a contribution leads to procrastination. To counter this, you must press for specific accomplishments within prescribed deadlines. In other words, to force action you need a campaign schedule with target dates understood by all. Everyone will then know the rules of the game and, despite the pressure, will be grateful for the deadline.

Failing to have a strong rationale.

Before setting out to raise money, each organization must think through the rationale for its appeal: why do the funds need to be raised, what will they achieve, and who will benefit? The mere fact that you and your board need money won't stir people, no matter how well organized your effort. Rather, with your case for support you must move your prospects emotionally and intellectually. They need to feel that, by contributing to your organization, life will in some way be better for them, for their children and grandchildren. They need to sense that their community - or even the nation - will be advanced as a result.

Failing to cultivate donors.

Cultivation, a sustained effort to inform and involve your prospects, is needed for practically every gift - the bigger the gift, usually the more preparatory steps needed. The best cultivation, which uses a mixture of printed matter, special events, and personal attention, takes place slowly over a period of time, sometimes years. If there's any secret to it, it is being yourself and cultivating people the way you would want to be cultivated. That is, with simple sincerity not glitzy programs. Donors give more when they can visualize an organization not as an organization but as people. Achieving that end is, in essence, the goal of all successful cultivation programs.

Failing to set a realistic goal.

In all but the newborn nonprofit, it's a mistake at the outset of a campaign to say, "We'll raise as much as we can." This often reveals to prospective donors that your board or staff haven't analyzed the organization's needs.

Rather, a tenable dollar goal emanates out of your organization's growth pattern and the (evaluated) financial ability of your prospect list. It is not, as some assume, simply a percentage increase over last year's gross, nor is it necessarily the difference between the total dollars you need, less expected income. While some argue for a high goal, and others insist on a low, achievable one, what really is desired is that magic number that inspires your volunteers, makes them work harder than they expected, and gives them the unmatched thrill of victory.

Failing to train solicitors adequately.

No matter how virtuous your project or organization, most prospects need to be sold on contributing. You must, therefore, have a team of highly trained solicitors - a "sales force" if you will.

Generally, you'll be dealing with three types of volunteers, each requiring slightly different treatment. First is the rookie who wants to help but needs detailed instructions. Second is the veteran of many campaigns who needs special prodding to attend trainings. And third is *every* volunteer who's being introduced to new procedures. No matter how bright or experienced your volunteers, nor how busy they are, too many drives degenerate due to mediocre solicitor training.

Failing to thank your donors.

Thanking donors, besides being polite, is an act of cultivation - and a smart one. People appreciate when their generosity is recognized. They not only feel closer to your organization, they're inclined to continue giving.

Most important with thank-yous is to acknowledge gifts positively and quickly. You want the donor to know that your trustees are aware of the gift, that his or her generosity will stir others to give, and that your organization will put the money to good use. Board members can be especially effective in expressing appreciation, either by sending notes or by making telephone calls to selected donors.

Failing to focus on your top prospects first.

It is foolish to squander your efforts on small donors until you've approached all of your best prospects. This is of course known as sequential solicitation.

You begin by seeking the largest gift first - the one (at the top of your Gift Table) that is needed to make your campaign a success. If this top gift comes in at the level you require, then it will set the standard and all other gifts will relate to it. If it's too low, other gifts will drop accordingly and possibly imperil your whole campaign. Sequential solicitation forces you to focus on your most promising prospects. While small donors are graciously treated, they do not receive disproportionate attention.

Failing to ask for a specific gift.

The need to ask for a specific gift is one of the most misunderstood - or is it feared? - principles in raising money. "Will you join me in giving $500 to the Wakefield Symphony?" leaves no doubt as to the size of gift the solicitor is requesting.

Most prospective donors need and want guidance. By requesting a specific amount, you show that you've given thought to your drive and you put the prospect in a position of having to respond. The suggested amount becomes a frame of reference, one that will get serious consideration if the solicitor is a friend, peer, or respected community figure.

Failing to concentrate on the best sources and the most productive methods.

Nearly every board hopes it can raise the money it needs from foundations and businesses. These sources, perhaps because they're more impersonal, are seen as less scary than people. And while, certainly, you want diversity in your funding, it's imperative that you and your board understand that most contributions - fully 90 percent - come from individuals. Here is where you'll invest your time and effort if you're serious.

As for methods, the most effective way of raising money - and most productive in terms of the *size* of gifts - is the face-to-face approach. The second most productive - again in terms of the *size* of gifts - is the appeal made to a small group of persons. The third most effective is the telephone call. And the least effective solicitation, in terms of gift size, is direct mail.

Failing to find the right person to ask.

Find the right person to ask the right person is an old but enduring maxim in fund raising. There will of course be exceptions, but a solicitor who makes a $100 commitment to your cause should call upon prospects who are capable of giving a similar amount. Likewise, a $500 prospect is best approached by a solicitor who himself has contributed a similar sum.

But as important as matching like amounts is pinpointing just the right solicitor. Some prospects expect to be asked by the president or the chairperson of the board. Others are less formal and would welcome the person they know best from the organization to ask for the gift. Still others may need the ego stroking of a team of solicitors. Reading this dynamic correctly is the *key* to success. In a large campaign, solicitor/prospect matching can consume hours. It is, however, one of the very best uses of time.

Failing to see your top prospects in person.

While there are dozens of ways to solicit prospects, nothing beats the personal request. The shopworn phrase, people give to people not to organizations, is another way of phrasing this principle. Certainly if your organization has a favorable image it helps. But the personal request of a friend or peer for support - this has a far greater impact than any knowledge your prospect may have about you.

Harold Seymour, fund raising guru, puts it best: "For clinking money, you can shake the can. For folding money, you should go ask for it. For checks and securities and gifts in pledges, you have to take some pains - make the appointment, perhaps take someone along, count on making two or more calls, and in general give the process enough time and loving care to let it grow and prosper."

The Mistakes

1. Thinking your organization will attract support simply because it's a good cause.
2. Thinking that others can raise the money for you.
3. Believing that because people are wealthy they will contribute to you.
4. Thinking you can whisk wealthy prospects in at the last minute.
5. Failing to research and evaluate prospects.
6. Failing to ask.
7. Thinking that publicity or written materials will raise money.
8. Failing to recruit the right trustees.
9. Believing you can raise money by the multiplication table.
10. Failing to have deadlines.
11. Failing to have a strong rationale.
12. Failing to cultivate donors.
13. Failing to set a realistic goal.
14. Failing to train solicitors adequately.
15. Failing to thank your donors.
16. Failing to focus on your top prospects first.
17. Failing to ask for a specific gift.
18. Failing to concentrate on the best sources and the most productive methods.
19. Failing to find the right person to ask.
20. Failing to see your top prospects in person.

FOUNDATIONS

ALABAMA

1
Alabama Power Foundation, Inc.
600 N. 18th Street
Birmingham, AL 35291
(205) 250-2393

Operating grants; Shakespeare Festival; American Lung Association; American Red Cross; Hospital Foundation; Boy Scouts; Family and Child Services; Children's Dance Foundation; Arts Foundation; Child Caring Foundation; Parents as Teachers; Neighborhood Growth; United Negro College Fund; Chamber of Commerce; Educational Television Commission; Public Library; Special Olympics; Board of Education; Literacy Coalition

Grants awarded to organizations located in Alabama.

2
J.L. Bedsole Foundation
c/o AmSouth Bank, N.A.
P.O. Box 1628
Mobile, AL 36629
(205) 432-3369

Operating grants; social welfare; higher education; hospitals; disabled; Public Library

3
Estes H. and Florence Parker Hargis Charitable Foundation
317 20th Street North
Birmingham, AL 35203
(205) 251-2881

Operating grants; Hargis Museum and Retreat; Boy Scouts; Ministries; Civic League; Fire Department; County Library; Alabama Family Alliance; Christian Fellowship; Church; YWCA

Typical grant range: $1,000 to $12,000

4
Hill Crest Foundation, Inc.
310 N. 19th Street
Bessemer, AL 35020
(205) 425-5800

Operating grants; health organizations; higher education; Churches; Ronald McDonald House; Alabama Institute for the Deaf and Blind; Meals on Wheels; Music Club; Child Caring Foundation; Family and Child Services; Literacy Center of Alabama; Presbyterian Children and Family Ministries; Community Health Center; Boys and Girls Club; Southeastern Bible; YMCA

Grants awarded to organizations located in Alabama.

Typical grant range: $3,000 to $25,000

5
M.W. Smith, Jr. Foundation
c/o AmSouth Bank, N.A.
P.O. Drawer 1628
Mobile, AL 36629

Operating grants; disabled; youth organizations; cultural organizations; environment

Typical grant range: $1,000 to $15,000

6
Sonat Foundation, Inc.
1900 Fifth Avenue North
P.O. Box 2563
Birmingham, AL 35202
(205) 325-7460

Operating grants; social welfare; disabled; health organizations; cultural organizations

Grants awarded to organizations located in areas of company operations.

Typical grant range: $3,000 to $20,000

ALASKA

7
Alaska Conservation Foundation
750 W. 2nd Ave., Suite 104
Anchorage, AK 99501
(907) 276-1917

Operating grants; environment

Grants awarded to organizations located in Alaska.

Typical grant range: $2,000 to $7,000

ARIZONA

8
Arizona Community Foundation
2122 E. Highland Avenue, Suite 400
Phoenix, AZ 85016
(602) 381-1400

Operating grants; disabled; community development; cultural organizations; youth organizations; social welfare; AIDS

Grants awarded to organizations located in Arizona.

Typical grant range: $500 to $14,000

9
J.W. Kieckhefer Foundation
116 E. Gurley Street
P.O. Box 750
Prescott, AZ 86302
(602) 445-4010

Operating grants; health organizations; environment; youth organizations; social welfare; cultural organizations; disabled; elderly

Typical grant range: $2,000 to $20,000

10
Margaret T. Morris Foundation
P.O. Box 592
Prescott, AZ 86302
(602) 445-4010

Operating grants; elderly; social welfare; cultural organizations; animal welfare; disabled; Community Development Care (for disadvantaged people)

Grants awarded to organizations located in Arizona.

Typical grant range: $1,000 to $21,000

11
Mulcahy Foundation
80 W. Franklin Street
Tucson, AZ 85701
(602) 622-6414

Operating grants; youth organizations; cultural organizations; social welfare

Grants awarded to organizations located in Arizona, with an emphasis in Tucson.

Typical grant range: $1,000 to $5,000

12
Del E. Webb Foundation
2023 W. Wickenburg Way
P.O. Box 20519
Wickenburg, AZ 85358
(602) 684-7223

Operating grants; hospitals; health organizations; disabled; child welfare

Typical grant range: $5,000 to $75,000

ARKANSAS

13
De Queen General Hospital Foundation, Inc.
P.O. Box 674
De Queen, AR 71832

Operating grants; disabled; youth organizations; Adult Activity Center

Grants awarded to organizations located in Sevier County.

14
Murphy Foundation
200 N. Jefferson Ave., Suite 400
El Dorado, AR 71730

Operating grants; youth organizations; health organizations; Ronald McDonald House; Center for Performing Arts; United Way; Art Center; Boys and Girls Club; Churches; Historical Foundation; Literacy Council; Friends of Public Radio; Women of the Arts; Police Department; Planned Parenthood

15
William C. and Theodosia Murphy Nolan Foundation
200 N. Jefferson, Suite 308
El Dorado, AR 71730
(501) 863-7118

Operating grants; social welfare; youth organizations

Grants awarded to organizations located in Arkansas.

Typical grant range: $500 to $8,000

16
Harold S. Seabrook Charitable Trust
c/o Worthen Trust Co.
P.O. Box 6208
Pine Bluff, AR 71611

Operating grants; social welfare; youth; recreation; cultural organizations

Grants awarded to organizations located in Arkansas.

Typical grant range: $1,500 to $7,000

CALIFORNIA

17
American Honda Foundation
P.O. Box 2205
Torrance, CA 90509
(310) 781-4090

Operating grants; youth organizations; minorities; higher education

Typical grant range: $15,000 to $75,000

18
ARCO Foundation
515 S. Flower Street
Los Angeles, CA 90071
(213) 486-3342

Operating grants; performing arts; social welfare; environment; youth organizations; minorities; homeless; elderly

Grants awarded to organizations located in areas of company operations.

19
Atkinson Foundation
1100 Grundy Lane, Suite 140
San Bruno, CA 94066
(415) 876-1359

Operating grants; disabled; homeless; elderly; minorities; child welfare; AIDS

Grants awarded to organizations located in San Mateo County.

Typical grant range: $2,000 to $12,000

20
Solomon R. & Rebecca D. Baker Foundation, Inc.
1900 Avenue of the Stars, Suite 630
Los Angeles, CA 90067
(213) 552-9822

Operating grants; disabled; hospitals; animal welfare; Autism Society of America; Foundation for the Junior Blind; Children's Hospital Society; Jewish Home for Aged; Legal Aid Society; American Cancer Society; Medical Center; Ranch for Boys; Volunteers of America

Grants awarded to organizations located in California.

21
Donald R. Barker Foundation
11661 San Vicente Blvd., Suite 300
Los Angeles, CA 90049

Operating grants; social welfare; youth organizations; hospitals; community development

Typical grant range: $2,000 to $11,000

22
Burton G. Bettingen Corporation
9777 Wilshire Blvd., Suite 611
Beverly Hills, CA 90212
(310) 276-4115

Operating grants; child welfare; youth organizations; social welfare; higher education

Typical grant range: $20,000 to $150,000

23
Clorox Company Foundation
1221 Broadway
Oakland, CA 94612
(510) 271-7747

Operating grants; disabled; cultural organizations; minorities; youth organizations; health organizations; women; child welfare; homeless; community development

Grants awarded to organizations located in areas of company operations, with an emphasis in the Oakland vicinity.

Typical grant range: $2,000 to $8,000

24
Community Foundation for Monterey County
P.O. Box 1384
Monterey, CA 93942
(408) 375-9712

Operating grants; social welfare; environment; youth organizations; disabled; elderly

Grants awarded to organizations located in Monterey County.

25
Compton Foundation, Inc.
525 Middlefield Road, Suite 178
Menlo Park, CA 94025
(415) 328-0101

Operating grants; environment; social welfare; cultural organizations

Typical grant range: $3,000 to $25,000

26
Joseph Drown Foundation
1999 Ave. of the Stars, Suite 1930
Los Angeles, CA 90067
(213) 277-4488

Operating grants; performing arts; health organizations; minorities; social welfare; homeless; women; child welfare; elderly; disabled; youth organizations

Grants awarded to organizations located in California.

Typical grant range: $10,000 to $75,000

27
First Interstate Bank of California Foundation
633 W. Fifth Street
707 Wilshire Blvd., 15th Floor
Los Angeles, CA 90017
(213) 614-3068

Operating grants; youth organizations; cultural organizations; social welfare; disabled; community development; health organizations

Grants awarded to organizations located in areas of company operations (California).

Typical grant range: $2,000 to $30,000

28
Fleishhacker Foundation
One Maritime Plaza, Suite 830
San Francisco, CA 94111
(415) 788-2909

Operating grants; Fine Arts Museum; Encore Theatre Company; Theatre Bay Area; Congregation Emanu-EL; Friends of Recreation and Parks; University of California-Cal Performances; University of San Francisco

Grants awarded to organizations located in the San Francisco vicinity.

Typical grant range: $1,000 to $15,000

CALIFORNIA

29
Flintridge Foundation
433 N. Fair Oaks Ave., Suite 200
Pasadena, CA 91103
(818) 449-6667

Operating grants; environment; cultural organizations; youth organizations

30
Fluor Foundation
3333 Michelson Drive
Irvine, CA 92730
(714) 975-6797

Operating grants; cultural organizations; health organizations; social welfare; community development

Grants awarded to organizations located in areas of company operations.

31
Foundation of the Litton Industries
360 N. Crescent Drive
Beverly Hills, CA 90210
(310) 859-5423

Operating grants; cultural organizations; community development; social welfare; disabled

Typical grant range: $1,000 to $20,000

32
Gap Foundation
One Harrison Street
San Francisco, CA 94105
(415) 291-2757

Operating grants; cultural organizations; youth organizations; AIDS

Most grants awarded to organizations located in the San Francisco vicinity.

Typical grant range: $500 to $15,000

33
Carl Gellert Foundation
2222 19th Avenue
San Francisco, CA 94116
(415) 566-4420

Operating grants; elderly; hospitals; women; disabled; youth organizations

Grants awarded to organizations located in the San Francisco vicinity.

Typical grant range: $1,500 to $9,000

34
Celia Berta Gellert Foundation
2222 19th Avenue
San Francisco, CA 94116
(415) 566-4420

Operating grants; social welfare; disabled; elderly; Foundation Center; University of San Francisco; Good Shepherd Grace Center; Holy Family Day Home

Grants awarded to organizations located in the San Francisco vicinity.

Typical grant range: $1,500 to $8,000

35
Fred Gellert Foundation
One Embarcadero Center, Suite 2480
San Francisco, CA 94111
(415) 433-6174

Operating grants; environment; youth organizations; disabled; elderly; health organizations; community development

Typical grant range: $2,000 to $8,000

36
Greater Santa Cruz County Community Foundation
2425 Porter Street, Suite 11
Soquel, CA 95073
(408) 662-8290

Operating grants; environment; community development; cultural organizations; social welfare; youth organizations; disabled

Grants awarded to organizations located in Santa Cruz County.

Typical grant range: $2,000 to $15,000

37
Josephine S. Gumbiner Foundation
P.O. Box 30656
Long Beach, CA 90853
(213) 439-9244

Operating grants; Long Beach Children's Museum; Teach America; YMCA; YWCA Women's Shelter; Casa Youth Shelter; United Cambodian Community; S.A. Association for Philanthropy; Legal Aid Foundation of Long Beach; Harbor Area Halfway Houses; Children's Home Society

Grants awarded to organizations located in Long Beach.

38
Walter and Elise Haas Fund
One Lombard Street, Suite 305
San Francisco, CA 94111
(415) 398-4474

Operating grants; cultural organizations; education; youth organizations; disabled

Grants awarded to organizations located in the San Francisco vicinity.

Typical grant range: $2,000 to $60,000

39
Luke B. Hancock Foundation
360 Bryant Street
Palo Alto, CA 94301
(415) 321-5536

Operating grants; youth organizations; homeless; minorities; disabled; cultural organizations; community development

Grants awarded to organizations located in the San Francisco vicinity.

Typical grant range: $2,000 to $25,000

40
Harden Foundation
P.O. Box 779
Salinas, CA 93902
(408) 442-3005

Operating grants; youth organizations; community development; elderly; social welfare; disabled; cultural organizations; animal welfare

Grants awarded to organizations located in the Salinas vicinity.

Typical grant range: $8,000 to $40,000

41
William and Flora Hewlett Foundation
525 Middlefield Road, Suite 200
Menlo Park, CA 94025
(415) 329-1070

Operating grants; environment; cultural organizations; child welfare; higher education; minorities; community development; AIDS

Grants awarded to organizations located in the San Francisco vicinity.

Typical grant range: $20,000 to $90,000

42
Lucile Horton Howe and Mitchell B. Howe Foundation
180 S. Lake Avenue
Pasadena, CA 91101
(818) 792-0514

Operating grants; social welfare; YMCA

CALIFORNIA

43
Jacobs Family Foundation, Inc.
P.O. Box 261519
San Diego, CA 92196
(619) 578-7256

Operating grants; Pasadena Neighborhood Housing Services

Typical grant range: $2,000 to $30,000

44
George Frederick Jewett Foundation
The Russ Building
235 Montgomery Street
San Francisco, CA 94104
(415) 421-1351

Operating grants; environment; social welfare; disabled; youth organizations; education; animal welfare; Churches

Typical grant range: $1,000 to $20,000

45
Karl Kirchgessner Foundation
c/o Greenberg, Glusker, Fields, Claman & Machtinger
1900 Ave. of the Stars, Suite 2100
Los Angeles, CA 90067
(213) 553-3610

Operating grants; disabled; elderly; youth organizations; health organizations

Grants awarded to organizations located in the Southern California vicinity.

Typical grant range: $5,000 to $40,000

46
Komes Foundation
1801 Van Ness Avenue, Suite 300
San Francisco, CA 94109
(415) 441-6462

Operating grants; hospitals; health organizations; disabled; minorities; elderly; youth organizations; social welfare

47
Koret Foundation
33 New Montgomery Street, Suite 1090
San Francisco, CA 94105
(415) 882-7740

Operating grants; disabled; elderly; homeless; social welfare; community development; health organizations; child welfare; cultural organizations; Jewish organizations

Typical grant range: $1,000 to $50,000

48
Louis R. Lurie Foundation
555 California Street, Suite 5100
San Francisco, CA 94104
(415) 392-2470

Operating grants; cultural organizations; community development; health organizations; AIDS

Typical grant range: $5,000 to $30,000

49
Bertha Ross Lytel Foundation
P.O. Box 893
Ferndale, CA 95536
(707) 786-4682

Operating grants; elderly; disabled; health organizations; performing arts; museum; social welfare

Grants awarded to organizations located in Humboldt County.

Typical grant range: $500 to $25,000

CALIFORNIA

50
Marin Community Foundation
17 E. Sir Francis Drake Blvd., Suite 200
Larkspur, CA 94939
(415) 461-3333

Operating grants; social welfare; cultural organizations; youth organizations; environment; employment projects; Marin Senior Coordinating Council; Novato Youth Center; Marin Conservation Corps.; Southern Marin Bible Institute; Ecumenical Convalescent Hospital Ministry of Marin; Marin Opera Company; Marin Mammal Center

Grants awarded to organizations located in Marin County.

Typical grant range: $5,000 to $200,000

51
Mattel Foundation
c/o Mattel Toys
333 Continental Blvd.
El Segundo, CA 90245
(310) 524-3530

Operating grants; Hugh O'Brien Youth Foundation; Junior Achievement; Peninsula Education Foundation; South Bay Literacy Council; American Heart Institute; Children's Diabetes Association; Pediatric AIDS Foundation; Sudden Infant Death Syndrome; Sickle Cell Association; California Institute of Technology; Boys and Girls Clubs; Easter Seals Society; Women's Shelter; Keep America Beautiful; Beach Cities Symphony; YWCA; United Way

52
McKesson Foundation, Inc.
One Post Street
San Francisco, CA 94104
(415) 983-8673

Operating grants; cultural organizations; all levels of education; social welfare; youth organizations; homeless; disabled; elderly

Grants awarded to organizations located in the San Francisco vicinity.

Typical grant range: $1,000 to $20,000

53
Samuel B. Mosher Foundation
3278 Loma Riviera Drive
San Diego, CA 92110
(619) 226-6122

Operating grants; hospitals; health organizations; cultural organizations; youth organizations

54
Peninsula Community Foundation
1700 S. El Camino Real, Suite 300
San Mateo, CA 94402
(415) 358-9369

Operating grants; cultural organizations; health organizations; homeless; child welfare; youth organizations; minorities; disabled; environment

Typical grant range: $1,000 to $20,000

55
Plum Foundation
P.O. Box 1613
Studio City, CA 91604
(818) 766-8064

Operating grants; Los Angeles Youth Programs; Family Health Center; All Saints AIDS Service Center; Caring for Babies with AIDS; McMaster University; Teach for America; American Oceans Campaign; Churches; Family Resource Center

Typical grant range: $5,000 to $30,000

CALIFORNIA

56
San Francisco Foundation
685 Market Street, Suite 910
San Francisco, CA 94105
(415) 495-3100

Operating grants; health organizations; environment; community development; elderly

Grants awarded in Alameda, Contra Costa, Marin, San Francisco, and San Mateo counties.

Typical grant range: $2,000 to $40,000

57
George H. Sandy Foundation
P.O. Box 591717
San Francisco, CA 94159

Operating grants; disabled; youth organizations; minorities

Grants awarded to organizations located in the San Francisco vicinity.

58
Stanley Smith Horticultural Trust
49 Geary Street, Suite 244
San Francisco, CA 94108
(415) 643-6264

Operating grants; horticultural related organizations; American Association of Botanical Gardens and Arboretum; Tree Consortium

Typical grant range: $5,000 to $30,000

59
Edward L. & Addie M. Soule Foundation
P.O. Drawer SS
Walnut Creek, CA 94596

Operating grants; hospice; Food Bank; Guide Dogs for the Blind; Juvenile Diabetes International Foundation; Bible Translators; Seminary; Oral School; Alzheimer's Services; Children's Brain Disease; Children's Hospital Foundation; Leukemia Society of America; California Burn Foundation; Salvation Army; Boy Scouts of America; Children's Home Society; YMCA; Foundation for Teaching Economics

60
James L. Stamps Foundation, Inc.
P.O. Box 250
Downey, CA 90241
(310) 861-3112

Operating grants; Protestant related organizations; Fellowship Youth Camps; Downey Symphonic Society

61
Jules and Doris Stein Foundation
P.O. Box 30
Beverly Hills, CA 90213
(310) 276-2101

Operating grants; cultural organizations; health organizations; hospitals; social welfare

Typical grant range: $2,000 to $15,000

62
Elbridge & Mary Stuart Foundation
c/o Bank of America
P.O. Box 3189, Terminal Annex
Los Angeles, CA 90051
(213) 613-4877

Operating grants; Shakespeare Festival; Child Abuse Prevention Foundation; Friends of Child Advocates; Hospital and Rape Treatment

CALIFORNIA

63
Stuart Foundations
188 The Embarcadero, Suite 420
San Francisco, CA 94105
(415) 495-1144

Operating grants; hospitals; health organizations; child welfare; disabled; animal welfare; all levels of education

Grants awarded to organizations located throughout California.

Typical grant range: $25,000 to $55,000

64
Morris Stulsaft Foundation
100 Bush Street
San Francisco, CA 94104
(415) 986-7117

Operating grants; social welfare; youth organizations

Typical grant range: $3,000 to $15,000

65
Times Mirror Foundation
Times Mirror Square
Los Angeles, CA 90053
(213) 237-3945

Operating grants; cultural organizations; youth organizations

Grants awarded to organizations located in areas of company operations, with an emphasis in Southern California.

Typical grant range: $7,000 to $75,000

66
Transamerica Foundation
600 Montgomery Street
San Francisco, CA 94111
(415) 983-4185

Operating grants; social welfare; cultural organizations; youth organizations; AIDS

Grants awarded to organizations located in the San Francisco vicinity.

Typical grant range: $1,000 to $20,000

67
Valley Foundation
333 W. Santa Clara Street
San Jose, CA 95113
(508) 292-1124

Operating grants; San Jose Museum of Art

Grants awarded to organizations located in the Santa Clara vicinity.

Typical grant range: $15,000 to $85,000

68
W.W.W. Foundation
1260 Huntington Drive, Suite 204
South Pasadena, CA 91030

Operating grants; hospice; orchestra; Episcopal Outreach; Humane Society; Animal Care Center; Park Foundation in Santa Barbara; Music Academy; Council on Alcoholism and Drug Abuse; Institute for Global Ethics; Thomas Jefferson Memorial Foundation; Brook Green Gardens; Ronald McDonald House; Hospital Foundation; YMCA

Grants awarded to organizations located in California.

Grants awarded to preselected organizations.

Typical grant range: $500 to $12,000

69
L.K. Whittier Foundation
1260 Huntington Drive, Suite 204
South Pasadena, CA 91030

Operating grants; high school; Friends of the Family; Legal Foundation; I Have A Dream; Friends of Valley Bookmobile; Education Fund; KCE-TV; Music Center; Theatre for Performing Arts; Homeless Women and Children

Grants awarded to organizations located in California.

Grants awarded to preselected organizations.

Typical grant range: $2,000 to $35,000

COLORADO

70
Anschutz Family Foundation
2400 Anaconda Tower
555 17th Street
Denver, CO 80202
(303) 293-2338

Operating grants; elderly; child welfare; health organizations; youth organizations

Typical grant range: $3,000 to $10,000

71
Boettcher Foundation
600 17th Street, Suite 2210 South
Denver, CO 80202
(303) 534-1937

Operating grants; cultural organizations; disabled; elderly; youth organizations; homeless; health organizations; child welfare; community development

Grants awarded to organizations located in Colorado.

Typical grant range: $5,000 to $45,000

72
Chamberlain Foundation
P.O. Box 5003
Pueblo, CO 81002
(719) 543-8596

Operating grants; Pueblo County Historical Society; Pueblo Ballet; Symphony; Fellowship of Christian Athletes Foundation; Wet Mt. Wildlife Rehab.; Boy Scouts of America; YMCA; Boys and Girls Club; Churches; Pueblo Suicide Prevention Center; Nature Center of Pueblo

Grants awarded to organizations located in Pueblo County.

Typical grant range: $2,000 to $8,000

73
Collins Foundation
c/o Norwest Bank, Boulder
P.O. Box 299
Boulder, CO 80306
(303) 441-0309

Operating grants; youth organizations; social welfare; health organizations

Typical grant range: $500 to $3,500

74
Adolph Coors Foundation
3773 Cherry Creek North Drive, Suite 955
Denver, CO 80209
(303) 388-1636

Operating grants; cultural organizations; community development; social welfare; youth organizations; homeless; minorities; hospice; health organizations; disabled

Grants awarded to organizations located in Colorado.

Typical grant range: $5,000 to $45,000

75
El Pomar Foundation
Ten Lake Circle
P.O. Box 158
Colorado Springs, CO 80901
(719) 633-7733

Operating grants; cultural organizations; zoos; hospice; health organizations; homeless; community development

Grants awarded to organizations located in Colorado.

Typical grant range: $3,000 to $50,000

76
Humphreys Foundation
555 17th Street, Suite 2900
Denver, CO 80202
(303) 295-8461

Operating grants; social welfare; health organizations; Garland Country Day School; Legal Aid Society; Vail Mt. School

Grants awarded to organizations located in Colorado.

Typical grant range: $500 to $4,500

77
A. V. Hunter Trust, Inc.
55 Madison Street, Suite 225
Denver, CO 80206
(303) 399-5450

Operating grants; social welfare; elderly; youth organizations

Most grants awarded to organizations located in Denver.

Typical grant range: $3,000 to $30,000

78
Helen K. and Arthur E. Johnson Foundation
1700 Broadway, Room 2302
Denver, CO 80290
(303) 861-4127

Operating grants; youth organizations; community development; health organizations; cultural organizations

Grants awarded to organizations located in Colorado.

Typical grant range: $12,000 to $100,000

79
Carl W. and Carrie Mae Joslyn Charitable Trust
c/o Bank One, Colorado Springs, N.A.
P.O. Box 1699, Trust Dept.
Colorado Springs, CO 80942
(719) 471-5115

Operating grants; elderly; Goodwill Industries; Cancer Hospital; Junior Achievement; YMCA; Assistance League School

Grants awarded to organizations located in El Paso County.

Typical grant range: $500 to $4,000

80
Needmor Fund
1730 15th Street
Boulder, CO 80302
(303) 449-5801

Operating grants; minorities; community development; environment; social welfare

Typical grant range: $2,000 to $20,000

81
Martin J. and Mary Anne O'Fallon Trust
2800 S. University Blvd., #61
Denver, CO 80210
(303) 753-1727

Operating grants; Colorado Women's Employment and Education

Grants awarded to organizations located in Colorado, with an emphasis in Denver.

Typical grant range: $1,000 to $6,000

82
Schramm Foundation
8528 W. 10th Avenue
Lakewood, CO 80215
(303) 232-1772

Operating grants; Children's Hospital; Society to Prevent Blindness; Girl Scouts; Little Sisters of the Poor; Mt. Zion Lutheran Church

Grants awarded to organizations located in Colorado.

Typical grant range: $1,000 to $15,000

83
H. Chase Stone Trust
c/o Bank One
P.O. Box 1699
Colorado Springs, CO 80942
(719) 471-5000

Operating grants; cultural organizations; education; animal welfare; Business of Art Center

Grants awarded to organizations located in El Paso County.

Typical grant range: $1,000 to $15,000

84
US WEST Foundation
7800 E. Orchard Road, Suite 300
Englewood, CO 80111
(303) 793-6648

Operating grants; all levels of education; community development; disabled; youth organizations; social welfare; minorities

Grants awarded to organizations located in areas of company operations.

Typical grant range: $3,000 to $20,000

CONNECTICUT

85
Fred R. & Hazel W. Carstensen Memorial Foundation, Inc.
c/o Tellalian & Tellalian
211 State Street
Bridgeport, CT 06604
(203) 333-5566

Operating grants; Greater Bridgeport Youth Symphony; United Congregational Church; Sacred Heart University

Grants awarded to organizations located in Connecticut.

86
Community Foundation of Greater New Haven
70 Audubon Street
New Haven, CT 06510
(203) 777-2386

Operating grants; social welfare; youth organizations; health organizations; community development

Grants awarded to organizations located in the New Haven vicinity.

Typical grant range: $2,000 to $40,000

87
Connecticut Mutual Life Foundation, Inc.
140 Garden Street
Hartford, CT 06154
(203) 727-6500

Operating grants; social welfare; all levels of education; cultural organizations; disabled; community development; AIDS

Grants awarded to organizations located in the Hartford vicinity.

Typical grant range: $1,000 to $20,000

88
Cyrus W. & Amy F. Jones & Bessie D. Phelps Foundation, Inc.
c/o Tellalian & Tellalian
211 State Street
Bridgeport, CT 06604
(203) 333-5566

Operating grants; Barnum Museum; Cabaret Theatre; Opera House; McGivney Community Center; International Institute of Connecticut; Habitat for Humanity; Inner-City Foundation for Charity and Education; Forman School; Armenian Church; WSHU Public Broadcasting

Grants awarded to organizations located in Connecticut.

89
Charles and Mabel P. Jost Foundation, Inc.
c/o Alexander R. Nestor
1140 Fairfield Avenue
Bridgeport, CT 06605

Operating grants; youth organizations; disabled; higher education; hospitals; child welfare; YMCA; Easter Seal Society; Salvation Army; Burn Core Foundation; Rehabilitation Center; Shriner's Hospital for Crippled Children; Hospital for Special Surgery; Historical Society; Theatre Company; Children's Home; Preparatory School

Grants awarded to organizations located in Connecticut.

Most grants awarded to preselected organizations.

90
Travelers Companies Foundation
One Tower Square
Hartford, CT 06183
(203) 277-1505

Operating grants; elderly; cultural organizations; youth organizations

Typical grant range: $15,000 to $120,000

DELAWARE

91
Borkee-Hagley Foundation, Inc.
P.O. Box 4590
Greenville, DE 19807
(302) 652-8616

Operating grants; homeless; elderly; social welfare; cultural organizations

Grants awarded to organizations located in Delaware.

Typical grant range: $1,000 to $5,000

92
Chichester duPont Foundation, Inc.
3120 Kennett Pike
Wilmington, DE 19807
(302) 658-5244

Operating grants; child welfare; cultural organizations; disabled; environment; health organizations

Typical grant range: $10,000 to $44,000

93
Crestlea Foundation, Inc.
1004 Wilmington Trust Center
Wilmington, DE 19801
(302) 654-2489

Operating grants; Academy of Music; Church Farm School; Cult Awareness Center; Community Services; Academy of Fine Arts; Maritime Museum; Museum of Art; Planned Parenthood; Free Library; Zoological Society of Philadelphia; Historical Society; SPCA

Grants awarded to organizations located in Delaware.

Typical grant range: $1,000 to $20,000

94
Raskob Foundation for Catholic Activities, Inc.
P.O. Box 4019
Wilmington, DE 19807
(302) 655-4440

Operating grants; homeless; women; child welfare; hospital; hospice; Catholic organizations

Typical grant range: $3,000 to $15,000

DISTRICT OF COLUMBIA

95
Morris and Gwendolyn Cafritz Foundation
1825 K Street, N.W., 14th Floor
Washington, DC 20006
(202) 223-3100

Operating grants; elderly; hospice; cultural organizations; community development; disabled; AIDS

Grants awarded to organizations located in the Washington, DC vicinity.

Typical grant range: $15,000 to $60,000

96
Queene Ferry Coonley Foundation, Inc.
P.O. Box 3722
Washington, DC 20007
(202) 333-3046

Operating grants; all levels of education; Health Services; Music Forum; Art Center; Foundation Center; Historical Society of Washington D.C.; Literacy Volunteers of America; Theatre Company; Refugee Centers; Urban Ministry; Housing Opportunities for Women; Child Development Center

Grants awarded to organizations located in the Washington, DC vicinity.

Typical grant range: $500 to $6,000

97
John Edward Fowler Memorial Foundation
1725 K Street N.W., Suite 1201
Washington, DC 20006
(202) 728-9080

Operating grants; youth organizations; higher education; elderly; disabled; homeless

Grants awarded to organizations located in the Washington, DC vicinity.

Typical grant range: $4,000 to $15,000

98
Freed Foundation
3050 K Street, N.W., Suite 335
Washington, DC 20007
(202) 337-5487

Operating grants; Women's Center of Monmouth County

Typical grant range: $2,000 to $30,000

99
Joseph P. Kennedy, Jr. Foundation
1350 New York Ave., N.W., Suite 500
Washington, DC 20005
(202) 393-1250

Operating grants; Down's Syndrome Adoption Exchange

Typical grant range: $10,000 to $70,000

100
Kiplinger Foundation
1729 H Street, N.W.
Washington, DC 20006
(202) 887-6559

Operating grants; cultural organizations; community development; hospitals

Grants awarded to organizations located in Washington, DC.

Typical grant range: $1,000 to $3,000

101
Eugene and Agnes E. Meyer Foundation
1400 Sixteenth Street, N.W., Suite 360
Washington, DC 20036
(202) 483-8294

Operating grants; homeless; community development; health organizations; social welfare

Grants awarded to organizations located in the Washington, DC vicinity.

Typical grant range: $12,000 to $35,000

102
Public Welfare Foundation, Inc.
2600 Virginia Ave., N.W., Room 505
Washington, DC 20037
(202) 965-1800

Operating grants; environment; social welfare; minorities; elderly

103
RJR Nabisco Foundation
1455 Pennsylvania Ave., N.W., Suite 525
Washington, DC 20004
(202) 626-7200

Operating grants; youth organizations; minorities; all levels of education

Typical grant range: $50,000 to $250,000

104
Alexander and Margaret Stewart Trust u/w of the late Helen S. Devore
First American Bank, N.A., Trust Dept.
740 Fifteenth Street, N.W.
Washington, DC 20005
(202) 637-7887

Operating grants; health organizations; Washington Hearing and Speech Society; Association for Retarded Citizens

Grants awarded to organizations located in the Washington, DC vicinity.

Typical grant range: $15,000 to $100,000

FLORIDA

105
Edyth Bush Charitable Foundation, Inc.
199 E. Welbourne Avenue
P.O. Box 1967
Winter Park, FL 32790
(407) 647-4322

Operating grants; social welfare; cultural organizations; disabled

Grants awarded to organizations located in central Florida.

Typical grant range: $15,000 to $65,000

106
Chatlos Foundation, Inc.
P.O. Box 915048
Longwood, FL 32791
(407) 862-5077

Operating grants; health organizations; social welfare; disabled; Christian organizations

Typical grant range: $3,000 to $30,000

107
Conn Memorial Foundation, Inc.
5401 Kennedy Blvd. West, Suite 530
Tampa, FL 33609
(813) 282-4922

Operating grants; youth organizations; San Antonio Boys Village

Grants awarded to organizations located in the Tampa vicinity.

Typical grant range: $2,000 to $20,000

FLORIDA

108
Jack Eckerd Corporation Foundation
P.O. Box 4689
Clearwater, FL 34618
(813) 398-8318

Operating grants; health organizations; hospitals; cultural organizations; community development

Grants awarded to organizations located in areas of company operations.

109
David Falk Foundation, Inc.
c/o SunBank of Tampa Bay
P.O. Box 1498
Tampa, FL 33601
(813) 224-2626

Operating grants; child welfare; disabled; elderly; health organizations

Grants awarded to organizations located in the Tampa vicinity.

110
Charles A. Frueauff Foundation, Inc.
307 E. Seventh Avenue
Tallahassee, FL 32303
(904) 561-3508

Operating grants; health organizations; hospitals; higher education; disabled; social welfare

Typical grant range: $10,000 to $35,000

111
Grace Foundation, Inc.
One Town Center Road
Boca Raton, FL 33486
(407) 362-1487

Operating grants; cultural organizations; minorities; hospitals; disabled

Grants awarded to organizations located in areas of company operations (W.R. Grace & Co.).

Typical grant range: $1,000 to $15,000

112
William M. & Nina B. Hollis Foundation, Inc.
P.O. Box 8847
Lakeland, FL 33806
(813) 646-3980

Operating grants; higher education; minorities; cultural organizations; youth organizations; social welfare; Churches

Most grants awarded to organizations located in Lakeland.

Typical grant range: $2,000 to $40,000

113
George W. Jenkins Foundation, Inc.
1936 George Jenkins Blvd.
P.O. Box 407
Lakeland, FL 33802
(813) 688-1188

Operating grants; health organizations; disabled; cultural organizations; youth organizations; social welfare

Grants awarded to organizations located in Florida.

Typical grant range: $500 to $25,000

114
John S. and James L. Knight Foundation
One Biscayne Tower, Suite 3800
2 S. Biscayne Blvd.
Miami, FL 33131
(305) 539-0009

Operating grants; cultural organizations; Haitian Refugee Center; American Press Institute; Children's Concert Society

Grants awarded to organizations located in areas of company operations (Knight-Ridder Newspapers).

Typical grant range: $10,000 to $125,000

FLORIDA

115
Alex & Agnes O. McIntosh Foundation
2511 Ponce de Leon Blvd., Suite 320
Coral Gables, FL 33134
(305) 444-6121

Operating grants; disabled; child welfare; social welfare; homeless; environment; youth organizations; AIDS

Typical grant range: $1,000 to $6,000

116
Paul E. & Klare N. Reinhold Foundation, Inc.
225 Water Street, Suite 2175
Jacksonville, FL 32202
(904) 354-2359

Operating grants; social welfare; health organizations; animal welfare; Johnny Appleseed Council; 4-H Club

Typical grant range: $1,000 to $20,000

117
M.E. Rinker, Sr., Foundation, Inc.
310 Okeechobee Blvd.
West Palm Beach, FL 33401

Operating grants; hospitals; all levels of education; Red Cross-Hurricane Relief; Churches

Grants awarded to organizations located in Florida.

Typical grant range: $15,000 to $125,000

118
United States Sugar Corporation Charitable Trust
c/o United States Sugar Corporation
P.O. Drawer 1207
Clewiston, FL 33440
(813) 983-8121

Operating grants; environment; social welfare; youth organizations; higher education; community development

Grants awarded to organizations located in Florida.

119
Wahlstrom Foundation, Inc.
2855 Ocean Drive, Suite D-4
Vero Beach, FL 32963
(407) 231-0373

Operating grants; disabled; elderly; cultural organizations; higher education

Typical grant range: $500 to $5,000

120
Joseph Weintraub Family Foundation, Inc.
200 S.E. First Street, Suite 901
Miami, FL 33131

Operating grants; Family Counseling Services; Boys and Girls Club; American Cancer Society; Trinity Episcopal School; Public Television-Channel 2; Greater Miami Jewish Federation; Plymouth Congregational Church; Miami Rescue Mission; Florida International University Foundation; Miami Lighthouse for the Blind; Miami Heart Institute; Salvation Army; Mt. Sinai Medical Center

Grants awarded to organizations located in Florida.

Typical grant range: $1,000 to $12,000

121
J. J. Wiggins Memorial Trust
P.O. Drawer 1111
Moore Haven, FL 33471
(813) 946-3400

Operating grants; Glade County Sheriff's Department; Girl Scouts; Boy Scouts; Moore Haven High School; Moore Haven Elementary School; City of Moore Haven

Grants awarded to organizations located in Glades County.

GEORGIA

122
Francis L. Abreu Charitable Trust
u/w of May P. Abreu
c/o Trust Co. Bank
P.O. Box 4655
Atlanta, GA 30302
(404) 588-7356

Operating grants; cultural organizations; social welfare; hospitals; disabled

Grants awarded to organizations located in Atlanta.

123
Fuller E. Callaway Foundation
209 Broome Street
P.O. Box 790
LaGrange, GA 30241
(404) 884-7348

Operating grants; youth organizations; community development; cultural organizations; health organizations; higher education; disabled; Churches

Most grants awarded to organizations located in the La Grange vicinity.

Typical grant range: $500 to $20,000

124
Coca-Cola Foundation, Inc.
One Coca-Cola Plaza, N.W.
Atlanta, GA 30313
(404) 676-2568

Operating grants; all levels of education; cultural organizations; community development

Grants awarded to organizations located in areas of company operations.

125
Robert and Polly Dunn
Foundation, Inc.
c/o Trust Co. Bank
P.O. Box 4655
Atlanta, GA 30302
(404) 588-7356

Operating grants; child abuse; youth organizations; social welfare

Most grants awarded to organizations located in the Atlanta vicinity.

Typical grant range: $1,000 to $12,000

126
Isobel A. Fraser & Nancy F. Parker
Charitable Trust
1530 Trust Co. Tower
Atlanta, GA 30303
(404) 658-9980

Operating grants; Atlanta Botanical Garden; Atlanta History Center; Fernbank Museum of Natural History; Atlanta Speech School; Crawford Long Hospital; Shepherd Spinal Center; Westminster Schools; Emory University; Stuttering Foundation of America; Salvation Army; Peachtree Presbyterian Church

Most grants awarded to organizations located in Atlanta.

Typical grant range: $3,000 to $20,000

127
Georgia Power Foundation, Inc.
333 Piedmont Avenue, 20th Floor
Atlanta, GA 30308
(404) 526-6784

Operating grants; elderly; social welfare; cultural organizations; homeless; health organizations; community development; disabled; youth organizations; minorities; higher education

Grants awarded to organizations located in Georgia.

Typical grant range: $2,000 to $25,000

128
John H. and Wilhelmina D. Harland Charitable Foundation, Inc.
Two Piedmont Center, Suite 106
Atlanta, GA 30305
(404) 264-9912

Operating grants; child welfare; disabled; social welfare; health organizations

Grants awarded to organizations located in Georgia, with an emphasis in Atlanta.

Typical grant range: $5,000 to $35,000

129
Walter Clay Hill and Family Foundation
c/o Trust Co. Bank
P.O. Box 4655
Atlanta, GA 30302

Operating grants; environment; cultural organizations; community development; social welfare; all levels of education; youth organizations; Churches

Grants awarded to organizations located in the Atlanta vicinity.

130
Ray M. and Mary Elizabeth Lee Foundation, Inc.
c/o NationsBank
P.O. Box 4446
Atlanta, GA 30302
(404) 607-4530

Operating grants; health organizations; hospitals; child welfare; cultural organizations

Most grants awarded to organizations located in the Atlanta vicinity.

Typical grant range: $2,000 to $25,000

131
Mattie H. Marshall Foundation
c/o Trust Co. Bank
P.O. Box 4655
Atlanta, GA 30302
(404) 588-8197

Operating grants; Humane Society; Sumter Regional Hospital; Women's Bridges of Hope; Andrew College; Asbury Theological Seminary; First United Methodist Church; Home for the Aging; Shepherd Spinal Center; Historic Preservation Society

132
Mauldin Foundation, Inc.
c/o Trust Co. Bank
P.O. Box 4655
Atlanta, GA 30302

Operating grants; Emory University; Columbia Presbyterian Church; Columbia Theological Seminary; Shepherd Spinal Center

Most grants awarded to organizations located in Georgia, with an emphasis in Atlanta.

133
Loretta Haley McKnight Charitable Trust Fund
First State Bank and Trust Co.
P.O. Box 8
Albany, GA 31702

Operating grants; higher education; Little Theatre; Girls, Inc.; Boys and Girls Club

Grants awarded to organizations located in Albany.

Typical grant range: $500 to $5,000

134
Metropolitan Atlanta Community Foundation, Inc.
The Hurt Building, Suite 449
Atlanta, GA 30303
(404) 688-5525

Operating grants; Techwood Baptist Center; Employment Project

Grants awarded to organizations located in the Atlanta vicinity.

Typical grant range: $2,000 to $15,000

135
Katherine John Murphy Foundation
c/o Trust Co. Bank
P.O. Box 4655
Atlanta, GA 30302
(404) 588-7356

Operating grants; health organizations; hospitals; cultural organizations; zoos

Most grants awarded to organizations located in Atlanta.

Typical grant range: $1,000 to $15,000

136
Oxford Industries Foundation, Inc.
222 Piedmont Avenue, N.E.
Atlanta, GA 30308
(404) 659-2424

Operating grants; higher education; Academy Theater; YMCA; United Way; Institute of Technology; Boy Scouts; Children's Hospital; Junior Achievement; Arts Festival; Friends of Zoo; Literacy Action; Leukemia Society of America; National Jewish Center; Parkinson's Disease Association; Stopping AIDS Together; American Red Cross; Chamber of Commerce; Kiwanis Foundation; Heart Research Foundation; Alumni Association-University; Committee Concerned for Children

137
Albert N. Parker Charitable Trust
c/o Trust Company Bank
P.O. Box 4655
Atlanta, GA 30302
(404) 588-8449

Operating grants; performing arts; cultural organizations; hospitals; Churches; Girl Scouts; YMCA; Empty Stocking Fund; United Way; Union Mission; American Diabetes Association; Salvation Army; School of Theology; Sheltering Arms; Juvenile Diabetes; National Illitis and Colitis Foundation; Children's Hospital; American Red Cross; American Cancer Society; American Heart Association

Most grants awarded to organizations located in Atlanta.

138
William A. Parker, Jr. Foundation
1530 Trust Co. Tower
Atlanta, GA 30303
(404) 658-9980

Operating grants; Emory University; Westminster Schools; Baptist Church; Peachtree Presbyterian Church; Atlanta Botanical Garden; Atlanta History Center; YMCA

Grants awarded to organizations located in Atlanta.

Typical grant range: $1,000 to $11,000

139
South Atlantic Foundation, Inc.
428 Bull Street
Savannah, GA 31401
(912) 231-3288

Operating grants; disabled; cultural organizations; social welfare; health organizations

140
Gertrude and William C. Wardlaw Fund, Inc.
c/o Trust Co. Bank
P.O. Box 4655
Atlanta, GA 30302

Operating grants; youth organizations; health organizations; social welfare

Grants awarded to organizations located in Atlanta.

Typical grant range: $2,000 to $15,000

HAWAII

141
Barbara Cox Anthony Foundation
1132 Bishop Street, No. 120
Honolulu, HI 96813

Operating grants; YMCA; Hawaii Meals on Wheels; Arthritis Foundation; Young People's Support Center; Volunteer Fire Department; American Cancer Society; N. Hawaii Community Hospital; Habitat for Humanity; Central Union Church; March of Dimes; Hawaii School for Girls; Scone Grammar School; American Red Cross; Planned Parenthood; Honolulu Academy of Arts; E. Maui Animal Refuge

Grants awarded to organizations located in Hawaii.

142
Atherton Family Foundation
c/o Hawaii Community Foundation
222 Merchant Street
Honolulu, HI 96813
(808) 537-6333

Operating grants; health organizations; social welfare; environment; cultural organizations; disabled; Churches; Hawaii Food Bank; Hawaii Youth at Risk; State of Hawaii, Department of Education

Grants awarded to organizations located in Hawaii.

Typical grant range: $2,000 to $20,000

143
Cooke Foundation, Limited
c/o Hawaiian Trust Co., Ltd.
P.O. Box 3170
Honolulu, HI 96802
(808) 537-6333

Operating grants; environment; animal welfare; child welfare; elderly; health organizations; social welfare; cultural organizations

Grants awarded to organizations located in Hawaii.

Typical grant range: $2,000 to $15,000

144
Mary D. and Walter F. Frear Eleemosynary Trust
c/o Bishop Trust Co., Ltd.
1000 Bishop Street
Honolulu, HI 96813
(808) 523-2234

Operating grants; social welfare; youth organizations; cultural organizations; health organizations; Churches

Grants awarded to organizations located in Hawaii.

Typical grant range: $1,000 to $8,000

145
Hawaii Community Foundation
222 Merchant Street
Honolulu, HI 96813
(808) 537-6333

Operating grants; environment; elderly; youth organizations; substance abuse; cultural organizations; community development; disabled; foster home; Hospice of Kona

Grants awarded to organizations located in Hawaii.

Typical grant range: $3,000 to $40,000

146
McInerny Foundation
c/o Bishop Trust Co., Ltd.
1000 Bishop Street
Honolulu, HI 96813
(808) 523-2234

Operating grants; hospice; social welfare; community development; disabled; youth organizations; cultural organizations

Grants awarded to organizations located in Hawaii.

Typical grant range: $5,000 to $20,000

147
Sophie Russell Testamentary Trust
c/o Bishop Trust Co., Ltd.
1000 Bishop Street
Honolulu, HI 96813
(808) 523-2233

Operating grants; animal welfare; disabled; health organizations; social welfare

Grants awarded to organizations located in Hawaii.

Typical grant range: $5,000 to $10,000

148
A. & E. Vidinha Charitable Trust
c/o Bishop Trust Co., Ltd.
1000 Bishop Street
Honolulu, HI 96813
(808) 523-2234

Operating grants; American Cancer Society; Easter Seal Society

Grants awarded to organizations located in Kauai.

Typical grant range: $6,000 to $30,000

IDAHO

149
Leland D. Beckman Foundation
c/o Holden, Kidwell, Hahn & Crapo
P.O. Box 50130
Idaho Falls, ID 83405

Operating grants; cultural organizations; social welfare; disabled; community development

Grants awarded to organizations located in Idaho Falls.

Typical grant range: $1,000 to $8,000

150
Roger and Sybil Ferguson Charitable Foundation
P.O. Box 519
Rexburg, ID 83440

Operating grants; Community Action Plan; Senior Citizens

Grants awarded to organizations located in Idaho.

Typical grant range: $500 to $5,000

151
Idaho Community Foundation
205 N. 10th Street, Suite 625
Boise, ID 83702
(208) 342-3535

Operating grants; hospice; homeless; sexual abuse; Public Library; Idaho Theatre for Youth; Idaho Hunger Action Council; Multiple Sclerosis Society; Boise Philharmonic Association

Grants awarded to organizations located in Idaho.

Typical grant range: $500 to $5,000

152
Harry W. Morrison Foundation, Inc.
3505 Crescent Rim Drive
Boise, ID 83706

Operating grants; Contribution Center of the Community

Grants awarded to organizations located in Boise.

Typical grant range: $500 to $10,000

153
Ray Foundation
P.O. Box 2156
Ketchum, ID 83340

Operating grants; disabled; hospice; Children's Trust Foundation; Cancer Lifeline; NW School for Hearing Impaired Children

Typical grant range: $3,000 to $30,000

ILLINOIS

154
American National Bank and Trust Company of Chicago Foundation
33 N. LaSalle Street
Chicago, IL 60690
(312) 661-6115

Operating grants; youth organizations; disabled; hospitals

Grants awarded to organizations located in areas of company operations, with an emphasis in the Chicago vicinity.

Typical grant range: $1,000 to $7,000

155
Amoco Foundation, Inc.
200 E. Randolph Drive
Chicago, IL 60601
(312) 856-6305

Operating grants; health organizations; hospitals; cultural organizations; social welfare; environment; disabled; youth organizations; higher education

Grants awarded to organizations located in areas of company operations.

Typical grant range: $4,000 to $60,000

156
AON Foundation
123 N. Wacker Drive
Chicago, IL 60606
(312) 701-3000

Operating grants; child welfare; disabled; cultural organizations; hospitals; health organizations

Grants awarded to organizations located in areas of company operations.

Typical grant range: $1,000 to $7,500

157
Bell & Howell Foundation
c/o Bell & Howell Co.
5215 Old Orchard Road
Skokie, IL 60077

Operating grants; social welfare; culture; community development; youth

Grants awarded to organizations located in areas of company operations.

158
Bersted Foundation
c/o Continental National Bank, N.A.
30 N. LaSalle Street
Chicago, IL 60697
(312) 828-8026

Operating grants; disabled; community development; health organizations; environment

Grants awarded in McHenry, DeKalb, Kane and DuPage Counties.

ILLINOIS

159
Blowitz-Ridgeway Foundation
2700 River Road, Suite 211
Des Plaines, IL 60018
(708) 298-2378

Operating grants; child welfare; disabled; minorities; youth organizations; AIDS

Grants awarded to organizations located in Illinois.

Typical grant range: $2,000 to $25,000

160
Helen Brach Foundation
55 W. Wacker Drive, Suite 701
Chicago, IL 60601
(312) 372-4417

Operating grants; animal welfare; disabled; elderly; environment

Typical grant range: $1,000 to $65,000

161
Brunswick Foundation, Inc.
One Brunswick Plaza
Skokie, IL 60077
(708) 470-4646

Operating grants; cultural organizations; youth organizations; disabled

Grants awarded to organizations located in areas of company operations.

162
Butz Foundation
c/o Northern Trust Co.
50 S. LaSalle Street
Chicago, IL 60675

Operating grants; disabled; cultural organizations; health organizations

Grants awarded to organizations located in Illinois.

163
Chicago Community Trust
222 N. LaSalle Street, Suite 1400
Chicago, IL 60601
(312) 372-3356

Operating grants; social welfare; women; disabled; performing arts; museums; elderly; homeless; AIDS; Mental Health Association; Metro Chicago Senior Foundation; Chicago-Area Alternative Education League; Donors Forum of Chicago; People's Music School; Literacy Chicago; Museum of Broadcast Communications

Grants awarded to organizations located in the Chicago vicinity.

Typical grant range: $15,000 to $70,000

164
Coleman Foundation, Inc.
575 W. Madison, Suite 4605-II
Chicago, IL 60661
(312) 902-7120

Operating grants; all levels of education; Helping Hand Rehabilitation; Lifeskills Foundation; Lions of Illinois Foundation; Center of Deafness; Rape Victims Advocates; Roseland Training Center; Child Center

Grants awarded to organizations located in the Chicago vicinity.

Typical grant range: $1,000 to $50,000

165
Doris and Victor Day Foundation, Inc.
1705 Second Avenue, Suite 424
Rock Island, IL 61201
(309) 788-2300

Operating grants; homeless; youth organizations; disabled; Illinois Migrant Council

Grants awarded to organizations located in the Illinois/Iowa Quad Cities.

Typical grant range: $1,000 to $15,000

ILLINOIS

166
Gaylord and Dorothy Donnelley Foundation
350 E. 22nd Street
Chicago, IL 60616
(312) 326-7255

Operating grants; environment; social welfare; child welfare; disabled; health organizations; animal welfare

Typical grant range: $1,000 to $5,000

167
Evanston Community Foundation
828 Davis Street, Suite 300
Evanston, IL 60201
(708) 475-2402

Operating grants; Mothers Against Gangs

Grants awarded to organizations located in Evanston.

Typical grant range: $1,000 to $12,000

168
Field Foundation of Illinois, Inc.
200 S. Wacker Drive, Suite 4
Chicago, IL 60606
(312) 831-0910

Operating grants; women; elderly; child welfare; health organizations; hospitals; homeless; community development; disabled

Grants awarded to organizations located in the Chicago vicinity.

Typical grant range: $5,000 to $45,000

169
First National Bank of Chicago Foundation
One First National Plaza
Chicago, IL 60670
(312) 732-6948

Operating grants; youth organizations; social welfare; community development

Grants awarded to organizations located in the Chicago vicinity.

170
Forest Fund
25060 St. Mary's Road
Libertyville, IL 60048
(708) 362-1994

Operating grants; child welfare; environment; social welfare; cultural organizations

Most grants awarded to organizations located in Chicago.

Typical grant range: $400 to $1,500

171
Harris Bank Foundation
111 W. Monroe Street
Chicago, IL 60603
(312) 461-5834

Operating grants; cultural organizations; youth organizations; minorities; higher education; women; social welfare; community development

Grants awarded to organizations located in the Chicago vicinity.

Typical grant range: $2,000 to $10,000

172
Harris Foundation
Two N. LaSalle Street, Suite 605
Chicago, IL 60602
(312) 621-0566

Operating grants; social welfare; disabled; child welfare; cultural organizations

Typical grant range: $500 to $8,000

173
Grover Hermann Foundation
c/o Schiff, Hardin & Waite
7200 Sears Tower, 233 S. Wacker Drive
Chicago, IL 60606
(312) 876-1000

Operating grants; health organizations; disabled; animal welfare

Typical grant range: $1,000 to $40,000

55

ILLINOIS

174
Joyce Foundation
135 S. LaSalle Street, Suite 4010
Chicago, IL 60603
(312) 782-2464

Operating grants; environment; all levels of education; minorities; disabled; youth organizations; community development

Typical grant range: $5,000 to $75,000

175
Charles G. and Rheta Kramer Foundation
c/o The Ross Group, Inc.
101 W. Grand Avenue, Suite 500
Chicago, IL 60610
(312) 527-4747

Operating grants; disabled; hospitals; health organizations; youth organizations; Jewish organizations

Typical grant range: $250 to $4,000

176
John D. and Catherine T. MacArthur Foundation
140 S. Dearborn Street
Chicago, IL 60603
(312) 726-8000

Operating grants; community development; cultural organizations; environment; women; animal welfare

177
Material Service Foundation
222 N. LaSalle Street
Chicago, IL 60601
(312) 372-3600

Operating grants; youth organizations; cultural organizations; community development; hospitals; health organizations

Grants awarded to organizations located in the Chicago vicinity.

178
Robert R. McCormick Tribune Foundation
435 N. Michigan Avenue, Suite 770
Chicago, IL 60611
(312) 222-3512

Operating grants; disabled; cultural organizations; homeless; child welfare; health organizations; minorities; women; youth organizations

Grants awarded to organizations located in the Chicago vicinity.

Typical grant range: $5,000 to $75,000

179
McGraw Foundation
3436 N. Kennicott Drive
Arlington Heights, IL 60004
(708) 870-8014

Operating grants; environment; social welfare; cultural organizations; health organizations

Grants awarded to organizations located in the Chicago vicinity.

Typical grant range: $2,000 to $30,000

180
Nalco Foundation
One Nalco Center
Naperville, IL 60563
(708) 305-1556

Operating grants; cultural organizations; hospitals; disabled; social welfare; youth organizations

Grants awarded to organizations located in areas of company operations.

Typical grant range: $1,000 to $12,000

ILLINOIS

181
**Northern Trust Company
Charitable Trust**
c/o The Northern Trust Company
Community Affairs Division
50 South LaSalle Street
Chicago, IL 60675
(312) 444-4059

Operating grants; disabled; community development; child welfare; minorities; women; homeless; cultural organizations

Grants awarded to organizations located in the Chicago vicinity.

Typical grant range: $1,500 to $12,000

182
Frank E. Payne and Seba B. Payne Foundation
c/o Continental Bank, N.A.
30 N. LaSalle Street
Chicago, IL 60697
(312) 828-1785

Operating grants; disabled; performing arts; animal welfare; hospitals; youth organizations; AIDS; Food Bank; Museums; American Red Cross; Recording for the Blind; Trinity Episcopal Church; Meals on Wheels; United Way; Literacy Council

Typical grant range: $10,000 to $95,000

183
Albert Pick, Jr. Fund
30 N. Michigan Avenue, Suite 819
Chicago, IL 60602
(312) 236-1192

Operating grants; community development; environment; social welfare; cultural organizations; health organizations

Grants awarded to organizations located in the Chicago vicinity.

184
Polk Bros. Foundation, Inc.
420 N. Wabash Avenue, Suite 204
Chicago, IL 60611
(312) 527-4684

Operating grants; social welfare; cultural organizations

Grants awarded to organizations located in the Chicago vicinity.

Typical grant range: $2,000 to $35,000

185
Relations Foundation
One E. Wacker Drive, Suite 2900
Chicago, IL 60601
(312) 321-5750

Operating grants; social welfare; Jewish related organizations

Grants awarded to organizations located in the Chicago vicinity.

186
Rockford Community Trust
321 W. State Street, 13th Floor
Rockford, IL 61101
(815) 962-2110

Operating grants; Tinker Swiss Cottage Museum; Family Consultation Service

Grants awarded to organizations located in the Rockford vicinity.

Typical grant range: $500 to $8,000

187
Sara Lee Foundation
3 First National Plaza
Chicago, IL 60602
(312) 558-8448

Operating grants; cultural organizations; child welfare; homeless; minorities; disabled; women; youth organizations

Most grants awarded to organizations located in the Chicago vicinity.

Typical grant range: $2,000 to $10,000

ILLINOIS

188
Square D Foundation
1415 S. Roselle Road
Palatine, IL 60067
(708) 397-2600

Operating grants; health organizations; hospitals; disabled; community development

Grants awarded to organizations located in areas of company operations.

Typical grant range: $1,000 to $7,000

189
Irvin Stern Foundation
116 W. Illinois Street
Chicago, IL 60610
(312) 321-9402

Operating grants; elderly; community development; homeless; minorities; disabled; Jewish organizations

Typical grant range: $4,000 to $20,000

190
Sunstrand Corporation Foundation
4949 Harrison Avenue
P.O. Box 7003
Rockford, IL 61125
(815) 226-6000

Operating grants; Boys and Girls Club; YMCA; Channel 10/36 Friends; Council on Economic Education; Children's Museum; Children's Home Society; Junior Achievement; Art Museum; Little League; Public Library; Literacy Service; Loma Symphony Orchestra; N. Illinois University; Special Olympics; United Negro College Fund; United Way

Grants awarded to organizations located in areas of company operations.

Typical grant range: $1,000 to $15,000

191
A. Montgomery Ward Foundation
c/o Continental Bank
30 N. LaSalle Street
Chicago, IL 60697
(312) 828-1785

Operating grants; youth organizations; hospitals; social welfare

Grants awarded to organizations located in the Chicago vicinity.

Typical grant range: $5,000 to $25,000

192
W.P. and H.B. White Foundation
540 Frontage Road, Suite 3240
Northfield, IL 60093
(708) 446-1441

Operating grants; social welfare; health organizations; hospitals; community development; youth organizations

Grants awarded to organizations located in the Chicago vicinity.

193
Wieboldt Foundation
53 W. Jackson Blvd., Suite 838
Chicago, IL 60604
(312) 786-9377

Operating grants; community development; minorities; environment

Most grants awarded to organizations located in the Chicago vicinity.

Typical grant range: $2,000 to $12,000

194
Woods Charitable Fund, Inc.
Three First National Plaza, Suite 2010
Chicago, IL 60602
(312) 782-2698

Operating grants; community development; cultural organizations; social welfare; homeless; youth organizations; disabled

Typical grant range: $10,000 to $35,000

INDIANA

195
John W. Anderson Foundation
402 Wall Street
Valparaiso, IN 46383
(219) 462-4611

Operating grants; disabled; youth organizations; health organizations; hospitals

Typical grant range: $5,000 to $30,000

196
Ayres Foundation, Inc.
6355 Morenci Trail
Indianapolis, IN 46268
(317) 299-2200

Operating grants; Associated Colleges of Indiana; Big Brothers; Boys and Girls Club; Education Foundation; Museum of Art; Music Society; Retirement Home; Friends of Holiday Park; Goodwill Industries; University Foundation; Library Foundation; Lighthouse Mission; Meals on Wheels; Churches; Health Foundation; Planned Parenthood; Salvation Army; St. Vincents New Hope; Food Bank; Visiting Nurse Association; Nature Conservancy

Grants awarded to organizations located in Indiana, with an emphasis in Indianapolis.

197
Ball Brothers Foundation
222 S. Mulberry Street
P.O. Box 1408
Muncie, IN 47308

Operating grants; social welfare; disabled; community development; recreation; cultural organizations; Christian Athletes Fellowship; Humanities Council; Indiana Office of Campus Ministries; Cultural Foundation; Therapeutic Riding; American Pianist Association

Grants awarded to organizations located in Indiana.

Typical grant range: $1,500 to $30,000

198
Robert Lee Blaffer Trust
P.O. Box 581
New Harmony, IN 47631
(812) 682-4431

Operating grants; Foundation for Historic Indiana; Youth Resource of Southwestern Indiana; Boys and Girls Club; Evansville Catholic School System; Episcopal Diocese of Indianapolis; Evansville Philharmonic Orchestra; Theater District, Inc.; Indiana University Foundation; Nature Conservancy

Grants awarded to organizations located in Indiana.

199
Clowes Fund, Inc.
250 E. 38th Street
Indianapolis, IN 46205
(317) 923-3264

Operating grants; cultural organizations; social welfare; disabled

Grants awarded to organizations located in Indianapolis.

Typical grant range: $3,000 to $40,000

200
Olive B. Cole Foundation, Inc.
6207 Constitution Drive
Fort Wayne, IN 46804
(219) 436-2182

Operating grants; disabled; youth organizations; Radio Reading Service

Typical grant range: $3,000 to $15,000

INDIANA

201
Foellinger Foundation
520 E. Berry Street
Ft. Wayne, IN 46802
(219) 422-2900

Operating grants; social welfare; cultural organizations; literacy; all levels of education; community development; recreation; health organizations; alcohol abuse; disabled; youth organizations; AIDS

Grants awarded to organizations located in the Ft. Wayne vicinity.

Typical grant range: $8,000 to $150,000

202
Ford Meter Box Foundation, Inc.
775 Manchester Ave.
P.O. Box 443
Wabash, IN 46992

Operating grants; higher education; social welfare; cultural organizations

Typical grant range: $500 to $10,000

203
Froderman Foundation, Inc.
18 S. Ninth Street
Terre Haute, IN 47807

Operating grants; youth organizations; Churches

Grants awarded to organizations located in Indiana.

Typical grant range: $2,000 to $15,000

204
Eugene and Marilyn Glick Foundation Corporation
P.O. Box 40177
Indianapolis, IN 46240
(317) 469-5858

Operating grants; cultural organizations; youth organizations; recreation; Jewish organizations

Grants awarded to organizations located in the Indianapolis vicinity.

205
Heritage Fund of Bartholomew County, Inc.
430 Second Street
P.O. Box 1547
Columbus, IN 47202
(812) 376-7772

Operating grants; youth organizations; social welfare; health organizations; all levels of education; Group Home for Boys; County Health Department; Youth Hope, Inc.

Grants awarded to organizations located in Bartholomew County.

206
Indianapolis Foundation
615 N. Alabama Street
Indianapolis, IN 46204
(317) 634-7497

Operating grants; disabled; elderly; cultural organizations; community development

Grants awarded to organizations located in the Indianapolis vicinity.

Typical grant range: $5,000 to $75,000

207
Arthur Jordan Foundation
1230 N. Delaware Street
Indianapolis, IN 46202
(317) 635-1378

Operating grants; child welfare; College of Fine Arts; Historic Landmarks Foundation; Museum of Art; Zoological Society; Life Leadership Development; YMCA; ARTS Indiana; Dance Kaleidoscope; Children's Choir/Opera; Symphony Orchestra; Meals on Wheels

Typical grant range: $3,000 to $15,000

208
Journal Gazette Foundation, Inc.
701 S. Clinton Street
Fort Wayne, IN 46802
(219) 461-8202

Operating grants; health organizations; youth organizations; social welfare; community development; hospitals

Typical grant range: $500 to $5,000

209
LGH Foundation, Inc.
R.R. 1
P.O. Box 332
Portland, IN 47371
(219) 726-7608

Operating grants; social welfare; youth organizations; cultural organizations; Humane Society; United Negro College Fund; American Red Cross; Evangelistic Association; Wee Care Child Care; Boy Scouts; Presbyterian Church; Center for Neurological Development

Most grants awarded to organizations located in Portland, Indiana.

Typical grant range: $500 to $3,000

210
Eli Lilly and Company Foundation
Lilly Corporate Center
Indianapolis, IN 46285
(317) 276-5342

Operating grants; community development; disabled; minorities; elderly; health organizations; cultural organizations

Grants awarded to organizations located in areas of company operations, with an emphasis in Indianapolis.

Typical grant range: $5,000 to $100,000

211
Lilly Endowment Inc.
2801 N. Meridian Street
P.O. Box 88068
Indianapolis, IN 46208
(317) 924-5471

Operating grants; cultural organizations; zoos; minorities; recreation; community development; youth organizations

Grants awarded to organizations located in Indiana, with an emphasis in Indianapolis.

Typical grant range: $2,500 to $60,000

212
Nicholas H. Noyes, Jr. Memorial Foundation, Inc.
Lilly Corporate Center
Indianapolis, IN 46285
(317) 276-3171

Operating grants; hospitals; youth organizations; zoo; disabled; Churches; Pioneer Settlement; Symphony Orchestra; Ballet Theatre; Children's Museum of Indianapolis

Grants awarded to organizations located in Indiana.

213
Plumsock Fund
9292 N. Meridian Street, Suite 312
Indianapolis, IN 46260
(317) 846-8115

Operating grants; cultural organizations; health organizations

Typical grant range: $1,000 to $15,000

214
M.E. Raker Foundation
6207 Constitution Drive
Fort Wayne, IN 46804
(219) 436-2182

Operating grants; Boys and Girls Club; Benet Learning Center

Grants awarded to organizations located in Indiana, with an emphasis in Fort Wayne.

215
Swisher Foundation, Inc.
7168 Graham Road, Suite 110
Indianapolis, IN 46250
(317) 849-0816

Operating grants; hospitals; health organizations; disabled; social welfare; youth organizations; cultural organizations

Typical grant range: $750 to $5,000

IOWA

216
Gardner and Florence Call Cowles Foundation, Inc.
715 Locust Street
Des Moines, IA 50309
(515) 284-8116

Operating grants; higher education; cultural organizations; social welfare; youth organizations; women

Grants awarded to organizations located in Iowa, with an emphasis in Des Moines.

Typical grant range: $20,000 to $85,000

217
Ralph & Sylvia G. Green Charitable Foundation
100 E. Grand Avenue, Suite 230
Des Moines, IA 50309

Operating grants; social welfare; performing arts; higher education; disabled; community development; hospitals; youth organizations

Grants awarded to organizations located in Des Moines.

218
Fred Maytag Family Foundation
200 First Street South
P.O. Box 426
Newton, IA 50208
(515) 792-1800

Operating grants; cultural organizations; health organizations; social welfare; disabled

Most grants awarded to organizations located in Newton and Des Moines.

Typical grant range: $2,000 to $30,000

219
Mid-Iowa Health Foundation
550 39th Street, Suite 104
Des Moines, IA 50312
(515) 277-6411

Operating grants; disabled; health organizations; elderly; youth organizations; social welfare

Most grants awarded to organizations located in Polk County.

KANSAS

220
Bank IV Charitable Trust
c/o Bank IV Kansas, N.A.
P.O. Box 1122
Wichita, KS 67201
(316) 261-4361

Operating grants; child welfare; disabled; elderly; health organizations; Kansas Food Bank Warehouse

Grants awarded to organizations located in areas of company operations (Kansas).

Typical grant range: $1,000 to $15,000

KANSAS

221
Baughman Foundation
P.O. Box 1356
Liberal, KS 67901
(316) 624-1371

Operating grants; disabled; youth organizations; cultural organizations; community development

Grants awarded to organizations located in Kansas, with an emphasis in Liberal.

Typical grant range: $1,000 to $20,000

222
Charles E. Carey Foundation, Inc.
P.O. Box 1488
Hutchinson, KS 67504

Operating grants; performing arts; recreation; American Red Cross; Central Christian Day Care; Emergency Shelter Home; Food Bank; Meals on Wheels; Horizons Mental Health; Hutchinson Art Association; Hutchinson Family Services; Boy Scouts; Elementary School; Sexual Assault/Domestic Violence Center

Grants awarded to organizations located in the Hutchinson vicinity.

223
Bruce G. Cochener Foundation
301 N. Main Street, Suite 1000
Wichita, KS 67202

Operating grants; Boy Scouts; Wichita Collegiate School; Univ. Congregation Church; Wichita Swim Club

Grants awarded to organizations located in Wichita.

224
DeVore Foundation, Inc.
P.O. Box 118
Wichita, KS 67201
(316) 267-3211

Operating grants; social welfare; disabled; youth organizations; health organizations; cultural organizations

Grants awarded to organizations located in the Wichita vicinity.

Typical grant range: $100 to $1,500

225
Fink Foundation
800 Bank IV Tower
Topeka, KS 66603
(913) 233-0541

Operating grants; health organizations; social welfare; St. John Lutheran Church; Blood Bank; St. Francis Hospital Foundation; American Red Cross

Grants awarded to organizations located in Kansas.

226
Olive White Garvey Trust
300 W. Douglas Street, Suite 1000
Wichita, KS 67202

Operating grants; higher education; American Printing House for the Blind; Young Men's Christian Association; National Association of Christian Churches; Historical Museum; United Way; Women in the Arts; Girl Scouts Council; Society for Crippled Children

Most grants awarded to preselected organizations.

227
Gault-Hussey Charitable Trust
c/o Bank IV Topeka, N.A., Trust Dept.
P.O. Box 88
Topeka, KS 66601
(913) 295-3463

Operating grants; social welfare; health organizations

Typical grant range: $500 to $5,000

228
Dane G. Hansen Foundation
P.O. Box 187
Logan, KS 67646
(913) 689-4832

Operating grants; youth organizations; health organizations; disabled

Typical grant range: $3,000 to $25,000

229
Henry Krause Charitable Foundation
P.O. Box 2707
Hutchinson, KS 67504
(316) 663-6161

Operating grants; American Red Cross; Boy Scouts; Girl Scouts; Hutchinson Hospital Foundation; Meals on Wheels; Interfaith Housing Services; Sexual Assault/Domestic Violence Center; Hutchinson Humane Welfare Association; Training Center for the Handicapped; United Way; YMCA; Salvation Army

Grants awarded to organizations located in Kansas.

Typical grant range: $1,000 to $10,000

230
Marley Fund
1900 Shawnee Mission Parkway
Mission Woods, KS 66205
(913) 362-1818

Operating grants; health organizations; community development; social welfare; child welfare

Grants awarded to organizations located in areas of company operations.

231
Powell Family Foundation
P.O. Box 7563
Overland Park, KS 66207
(913) 967-4321

Operating grants; youth organizations; community development

Grants awarded to organizations located in the Kansas City vicinity.

Typical grant range: $1,000 to $25,000

232
Yellow Corporate Foundation
P.O. Box 7563
Overland Park, KS 66207
(913) 344-4352

Operating grants; cultural organizations; social welfare; health organizations

Most grants awarded to organizations located in the Kansas City vicinity.

KENTUCKY

233
Foundation for the Tri-State Community, Inc.
P.O. Box 2096
Ashland, KY 41105
(606) 324-3888

Operating grants; Paramount Arts Center

234
Louisville Community Foundation, Inc.
325 W. Main Street, Suite 1110
Louisville, KY 40202
(502) 585-4649

Operating grants; disabled; elderly; environment; social welfare; community development

Grants awarded to organizations located in Louisville.

Typical grant range: $3,000 to $10,000

235
Herman H. Nettelroth Fund
c/o PNC Bank
Kentucky Citizens Plaza
Louisville, KY 40296

Operating grants; Metro United Way; Louisville Nature and Conservation Center

Grants awarded to organizations located in Jefferson County.

Typical grant range: $4,000 to $15,000

236
Norton Foundation, Inc.
4350 Brownsboro Road, Suite 133
Louisville, KY 40207
(502) 893-9549

Operating grants; social welfare; cultural organizations; youth organizations; homeless; environment; disabled

Grants awarded to organizations located in the Louisville vicinity.

Typical grant range: $3,000 to $25,000

237
Reed Foundation
P.O. Box 67
Gilbertsville, KY 42044

Operating grants; all levels of education; youth organizations; disabled

Typical grant range: $1,000 to $12,000

238
E.O. Robinson Mountain Fund
P.O. Box 54930
Lexington, KY 40555
(606) 233-0817

Operating grants; youth organizations; higher education; health organizations; disabled; hospitals

Typical grant range: $3,000 to $25,000

LOUISIANA

239
Joe W. and Dorothy Dorsett Brown Foundation
1801 Pere Marquette Building
New Orleans, LA 70112
(504) 522-4233

Operating grants; hospitals; health organizations; social welfare; women; community development; youth organizations; disabled

Grants awarded to organizations located in Louisiana.

240
Community Foundation of Shreveport-Bossier
401 Edwards Street, Suite 517
Shreveport, LA 71101
(318) 221-0582

Operating grants; museums; Boy Scouts; Biomedical Research Foundation of Northwest Louisiana

241
Frazier Foundation, Inc.
P.O. Box 1175
Minden, LA 71055
(318) 377-0182

Operating grants; disabled; child welfare; Christian organizations

Typical grant range: $5,000 to $15,000

242
Huie-Dellmon Trust
P.O. Box 330
Alexandria, LA 71301

Operating grants; hospitals; secondary education; higher education; social welfare

243
Lupin Foundation
3715 Prytania Street, Suite 307
New Orleans, LA 70115
(504) 897-6125

Operating grants; cultural organizations; disabled; community development

Grants awarded to organizations located in Louisiana.

244
Salmen Family Foundation
431 Gravier Street, Suite 400
New Orleans, LA 70130
(504) 581-6084

Operating grants; social welfare; youth organizations; elderly

Grants awarded to organizations located in Louisiana.

245
Fred B. and Ruth B. Zigler Foundation
P.O. Box 986
Jennings, LA 70546
(318) 824-2413

Operating grants; disabled; youth organizations; elderly; health organizations

Typical grant range: $500 to $8,000

MAINE

246
George P. Davenport Trust Fund
55 Front Street
Bath, ME 04530
(207) 443-3431

Operating grants; social welfare; community development; disabled

Grants awarded to organizations located in Bath.

Typical grant range: $1,000 to $20,000

247
Simmons Foundation, Inc.
One Canal Plaza
Portland, ME 04101
(207) 774-2635

Operating grants; Habitat for Humanity

Grants awarded to organizations located in Portland, Maine.

Typical grant range: $1,500 to $5,000

248
Warren Memorial Foundation
29 Hillview Road
Gorham, ME 04038
(207) 839-8744

Operating grants; child welfare; Maine Cancer Research; WCBB

Grants awarded to organizations located in Maine.

Typical grant range: $500 to $2,000

MARYLAND

249
Charles S. Abell Foundation, Inc.
8401 Connecticut Avenue
Chevy Chase, MD 20815
(301) 652-2224

Operating grants; women; disabled; homeless; child welfare; St. Gertrude's School

Typical grant range: $5,000 to $30,000

250
Alex Brown and Sons Charitable Foundation, Inc.
c/o Alex Brown and Sons, Inc.
135 E. Baltimore Street
Baltimore, MD 21202

Operating grants; social welfare; cultural organizations; health organizations; disabled

Grants awarded to organizations located in Maryland.

251
Columbia Foundation
10221 Wineopin Circle
Columbia, MD 21044
(301) 730-7840

Operating grants; disabled; health organizations; cultural organizations; social welfare; youth organizations

Grants awarded to organizations located in Howard County.

252
Marion I. and Henry J. Knott Foundation, Inc.
3904 Hickory Avenue
Baltimore, MD 21211
(410) 235-7068

Operating grants; cultural organizations; social welfare; higher education; community development; Maryland Food Bank; Save Our Streams; Shock Trauma Research Fund; Special Olympics; Maryland Dentistry for the Handicapped; Women's Housing Coalition; Habitat for Humanity; Choice Jobs Program; Child Advocacy Network

Typical grant range: $1,000 to $25,000

253
PHH Foundation, Inc.
11333 McCormick Road
Hunt Valley, MD 21031
(410) 771-2733

Operating grants; community development; disabled; health organizations; social welfare; cultural organizations

Grants awarded to organizations located in the Baltimore vicinity.

Typical grant range: $1,000 to $20,000

254
Aaron Straus and Lillie Straus Foundation, Inc.
101 W. Mt. Royal Avenue
Baltimore, MD 21201
(301) 539-8308

Operating grants; child welfare; cultural organizations; disabled; Jewish organizations

Grants awarded to organizations located in the Baltimore vicinity.

Typical grant range: $1,500 to $50,000

255
Weir Foundation Trust
1320 Fenwick Lane, Suite 700
Silver Spring, MD 20910

Operating grants; hospitals; hospice; Boys Clubs/Boys and Girls Club; Youth Soccer/Youth League; Salvation Army; Planned Parenthood; United Action for the Elderly; United Way; United Cerebral Palsy; Historic Annapolis; Churches

Most grants awarded to preselected organizations.

MASSACHUSETTS

256
Adelaide Breed Bayrd Foundation
28 Pilgrim Road
Melrose, MA 02176
(617) 662-7342

Operating grants; cultural organizations; health organizations; social welfare; community development

Grants awarded to organizations located in the Malden vicinity.

Typical grant range: $1,000 to $15,000

MASSACHUSETTS

257
Boston Edison Foundation
800 Boylston Street
Boston, MA 02199
(617) 424-2235

Operating grants; community development; cultural organizations; social welfare; health organizations; hospitals; youth organizations

Grants awarded to organizations located in areas of company operations, with an emphasis in Boston.

Typical grant range: $1,000 to $15,000

258
Boston Globe Foundation II, Inc.
The Boston Globe Building
135 Morrissey Blvd.
Boston, MA 02107
(617) 929-2895

Operating grants; community development; health organizations; youth organizations; cultural organizations; disabled

Grants awarded to organizations located in the Boston vicinity.

Typical grant range: $3,000 to $20,000

259
Alexander H. Bright Charitable Trust
c/o Boston Safe Deposit & Trust Co.
One Boston Place
Boston, MA 02108
(617) 722-7337

Operating grants; environment; social welfare; youth organizations

Most grants awarded to organizations located in Massachusetts.

Typical grant range: $300 to $2,500

260
Bushrod H. Campbell and Adah F. Hall Charity Fund
c/o Palmer & Dodge
One Beacon Street
Boston, MA 02108
(617) 573-0328

Operating grants; elderly; disabled; health organizations

Grants awarded to organizations located in the Boston vicinity.

Typical grant range: $2,000 to $10,000

261
Roberta M. Childs Charitable Foundation
P.O. Box 639
North Andover, MA 01845

Operating grants; child welfare; disabled; hospitals; health organizations; homeless

Grants awarded to organizations located in Massachusetts.

Typical grant range: $1,000 to $5,000

262
Clark Charitable Trust
P.O. Box 251
Lincoln, MA 01773

Operating grants; environment; animal welfare; social welfare

263
Clipper Ship Foundation, Inc.
c/o Hill & Barlow, 100 Oliver Street
One International Plaza, 20th Floor
Boston, MA 02110
(617) 439-3555

Operating grants; disabled; minorities; homeless; elderly; child welfare

Grants awarded to organizations located in the Boston vicinity.

Typical grant range: $2,000 to $15,000

MASSACHUSETTS

264
Lillian L. and Harry A. Cowan Foundation Corporation
20 Chapel Street, #412-B
Brookline, MA 02146
(617) 738-1461

Operating grants; disabled; elderly; child welfare; health organizations

Grants awarded to organizations located in the Boston vicinity.

Typical grant range: $3,000 to $7,000

265
Fred Harris Daniels Foundation, Inc.
c/o The Mechanics Bank, Trust Dept.
P.O. Box 15073
Worcester, MA 01615
(508) 798-6467

Operating grants; cultural organizations; environment; social welfare; community development

Most grants awarded to organizations located in the Worcester vicinity.

Typical grant range: $1,000 to $30,000

266
Ruth H. and Warren A. Ellsworth Foundation
370 Main Street, 12th Floor
Worcester, MA 01608
(508) 798-8621

Operating grants; health organizations; youth organizations; New England Science Center; Old Sturbridge Village

Grants awarded to organizations located in the Worcester vicinity.

Typical grant range: $2,000 to $25,000

267
Francis A. & Jacquelyn H. Harrington Foundation
370 Main Street, Suite 1200
Worcester, MA 01608
(508) 798-8621

Operating grants; Worcester Historical Museum; WICN

Grants awarded to organizations located in the Worcester vicinity.

268
Hyams Foundation
One Boston Place, 32nd Floor
Boston, MA 02108
(617) 720-2238

Operating grants; community development; elderly; youth organizations; social welfare; homeless

Typical grant range: $5,000 to $30,000

269
Island Foundation, Inc.
589 Mill Street
Marion, MA 02738
(508) 748-2809

Operating grants; community development; women; youth organizations; environment

Typical grant range: $2,000 to $15,000

270
Arthur D. Little Foundation
25 Acorn Park
Cambridge, MA 02140
(617) 498-5524

Operating grants; community development; cultural organizations; social welfare; minorities; environment; disabled; youth organizations

Grants awarded to organizations located in areas of company operations (Arthur D. Little, Inc.), with an emphasis in Cambridge.

Typical grant range: $1,500 to $5,000

MASSACHUSETTS

271
Morgan-Worcester, Inc.
15 Belmont Street
Worcester, MA 01605
(508) 755-6111

Operating grants; environment; cultural organizations; community development

Grants awarded to organizations located in the Worcester vicinity.

Typical grant range: $100 to $4,000

272
Norton Company Foundation
New Bond Street
P.O. Box 15008
Worcester, MA 01615
(508) 795-4770

Operating grants; cultural organizations; social welfare; youth organizations; all levels of education

Grants awarded to organizations located in areas of company operations.

Typical grant range: $500 to $3,000

273
Perpetual Trust for Charitable Giving
c/o Fleet Bank of Massachusetts, N.A.
75 State Street, 7th Floor
Boston, MA 02109
(617) 346-2467

Operating grants; anti-crime program; American Cancer Society; YMCA; St. Elizabeth's Hospital; Perkins School for the Blind

Grants awarded to organizations located in Massachusetts.

274
Polaroid Foundation, Inc.
750 Main Street, 2M
Cambridge, MA 02139
(617) 577-4035

Operating grants; social welfare; women; disabled; homeless; youth organizations; hospice; health organizations; cultural organizations; community development; AIDS

Grants awarded to organizations located in Massachusetts.

Typical grant range: $1,000 to $12,000

275
A.C. Ratshesky Foundation
38 Concord Avenue
Cambridge, MA 02138
(617) 547-4590

Operating grants; women; child welfare; minorities; social welfare; youth organizations; cultural organizations; community development

276
William E. Schrafft and Bertha E. Schrafft Charitable Trust
One Financial Center, 26th Floor
Boston, MA 02111
(617) 457-7327

Operating grants; hospitals; cultural organizations; community development; youth organizations; all levels of education; minorities

Most grants awarded to organizations located in the Boston vicinity.

Typical grant range: $3,000 to $20,000

277
Gardiner Howland Shaw Foundation
95 Berkeley Street, Suite 403
Boston, MA 02116
(617) 451-9206

Operating grants; women; youth organizations; community development; Crime and Justice Foundation; Social Justice for Women; Massachusetts Advocacy Center; Massachusetts Halfway Houses

Typical grant range: $4,000 to $9,000

278
State Street Foundation
c/o State Street Bank and Trust Co.
P.O. Box 351
Boston, MA 02101
(617) 654-3381

Operating grants; community development; social welfare; health organizations; cultural organizations; minorities; youth organizations

Grants awarded to organizations located in the Boston vicinity.

Typical grant range: $5,000 to $75,000

279
Abbot and Dorothy Stevens Foundation
P.O. Box 111
N. Andover, MA 01845
(508) 688-7211

Operating grants; environment; cultural organizations; youth organizations; social welfare; community development

Grants awarded to organizations located in Massachusetts.

Typical grant range: $2,000 to $10,000

280
Nathaniel and Elizabeth P. Stevens Foundation
P.O. Box 111
N. Andover, MA 01845
(508) 688-7211

Operating grants; health organizations; cultural organizations; environment; social welfare

Typical grant range: $1,000 to $11,000

281
Stride Rite Charitable Foundation, Inc.
c/o The Stride Rite Corporation
Five Cambridge Center
Cambridge, MA 02142
(617) 491-8800

Operating grants; child welfare; cultural organizations

282
Blanche M. Walsh Charity Trust
174 Central Street, Suite 329
Lowell, MA 01852
(508) 454-5654

Operating grants; social welfare

Grants awarded to Catholic related organizations.

Typical grant range: $500 to $3,000

283
Edwin S. Webster Foundation
Grants Management Associates, Inc.
230 Congress Street, 3rd Floor
Boston, MA 02110
(617) 426-7172

Operating grants; community development; youth organizations; cultural organizations; minorities

Most grants awarded to organizations located in the Boston vicinity.

MICHIGAN

284
ANR Foundation, Inc.
One Woodward Avenue
Detroit, MI 48226
(313) 965-1200

Operating grants; health organizations; community development; higher education; social welfare; disabled; women; youth organizations; recreation

Most grants awarded to organizations located in Detroit.

Typical grant range: $1,000 to $20,000

285
Barstow Foundation
c/o Chemical Bank
333 E. Main Street
Midland, MI 48640
(517) 631-9200

Operating grants; Habitat for Humanity; CARE; UNICEF; Cumberland College

286
Battle Creek Community Foundation
One Riverwalk Center
34 W. Jackson Street
Battle Creek, MI 49017
(616) 962-2181

Operating grants; Battle Creek Area Mathematics and Science Center; Southwest Michigan Funding Resource Center

Grants awarded to organizations located in the Battle Creek vicinity.

Typical grant range: $1,000 to $20,000

287
Bauervic-Paisley Foundation
2855 Coolidge Highway, Suite 100
Troy, MI 48084

Operating grants; secondary education; cultural organizations; health organizations

Typical grant range: $1,000 to $15,000

288
Besser Foundation
123 N. Second Avenue, Suite 4
Alpena, MI 49707
(517) 354-4722

Operating grants; higher education; youth organizations; social welfare; child welfare; cultural organizations

Most grants awarded to organizations located in Alpena.

Typical grant range: $4,000 to $50,000

289
A.G. Bishop Charitable Trust
c/o NBD Bank, N.A.
One E. First Street
Flint, MI 48502
(313) 760-8451

Operating grants; youth organizations; community development; social welfare; cultural organizations; health organizations

290
Samuel Higby Camp Foundation
145 S. Jackson
Jackson, MI 49201
(517) 787-4100

Operating grants; child welfare; social welfare; youth organizations; cultural organizations

Grants awarded to organizations located in Jackson County.

Typical grant range: $1,500 to $5,000

291
Clarence and Grace Chamberlin Foundation
600 Woodbridge Place
Detroit, MI 48226
(313) 567-1000

Operating grants; disabled; child welfare; all levels of education; hospitals; health organizations; elderly; social welfare; cultural organizations

Most grants awarded to organizations located in Michigan.

MICHIGAN

292
Community Foundation for Northeast Michigan
123 Water Street
Alpena, MI 49707
(517) 354-6881

Operating grants; museum; Big Brothers/Big Sisters

Grants awarded to organizations located in the Alpena County vicinity.

Typical grant range: $400 to $5,000

293
Community Foundation for Southeastern Michigan
333 W. Fort Street, Suite 2010
Detroit, MI 48226
(313) 961-6675

Operating grants; social welfare; youth organizations; child welfare; disabled; community development; Churches; Michigan Cancer Foundation; Planned Parenthood; Child and Family Services of Michigan; Salvation Army

Grants awarded in the following Counties: Wayne, Oakland, Macomb, Washtenaw, St. Clair, Monroe, Livingston.

Typical grant range: $1,000 to $25,000

294
Dorothy U. Dalton Foundation, Inc.
c/o Arcadia Bank
P.O. Box 50566
Kalamazoo, MI 49003

Operating grants; disabled; hospitals; cultural organizations; social welfare; youth organizations; community development; Youth Ministry

Grants awarded to organizations located in Kalamazoo County.

Typical grant range: $5,000 to $30,000

295
Helen L. DeRoy Foundation
3274 Penobscot Building
Detroit, MI 48226
(313) 961-3814

Operating grants; Jewish related organizations including social welfare

Grants awarded to organizations located in Michigan.

296
Detroit Edison Foundation
2000 Second Avenue, #642 WCB
Detroit, MI 48226
(313) 237-9271

Operating grants; social welfare; all levels of education; hospitals; youth organizations; cultural organizations; disabled

Grants awarded to organizations located in areas of company operations.

Typical grant range: $3,000 to $20,000

297
Alden & Vada Dow Fund
315 Post Street
Midland, MI 48640
(517) 835-6761

Operating grants; Shelter House; Star Commonwealth Schools; Big Brothers and Big Sisters; Midland County Child Protection Council; Albion College; College Foundation; Salvation Army; International Diabetes Center; Arts Foundation of Michigan; Midland Historical Society; Midland Music Society; Theatre Guild; Boy Scouts; Youth Development Corp.

Grants awarded to organizations located in Midland County.

MICHIGAN

298
Fibre Converters Foundation, Inc.
P.O. Box 117
125 East Broadway
Three Rivers, MI 49093

Operating grants; Salvation Army; American Red Cross; American Cancer Society; Food Bank; Fire Council/Police; Disabled American Veterans; Association for Emotionally Disturbed Children; American Heart Association; American Lung Association; Special Olympics

Grants awarded to organizations located in Michigan.

299
Fremont Area Foundation
108 South Stewart
Fremont, MI 49412
(616) 924-5350

Operating grants; cultural organizations; social welfare; health organizations; community development; elderly

Grants awarded to organizations located in Newaygo County.

Typical grant range: $2,000 to $20,000

300
General Motors Foundation, Inc.
13-145 General Motors Building
3044 W. Grand Blvd.
Detroit, MI 48202
(313) 556-4260

Operating grants; social welfare; higher education; minorities; cultural organizations; community development

Grants awarded to organizations located in areas of company operations.

Typical grant range: $2,000 to $125,000

301
Irving S. Gilmore Foundation
136 E. Michigan Avenue, Suite 615
Kalamazoo, MI 49007
(616) 342-6411

Operating grants; higher education; cultural organizations; youth organizations; community development

Grants awarded to organizations located in the Kalamazoo vicinity.

Typical grant range: $20,000 to $150,000

302
James and Lynelle Holden Fund
802 E. Big Beaver
Troy, MI 48083

Operating grants; youth organizations; elderly; performing arts; minorities; child welfare; disabled; social welfare; health organizations; hospital; animal welfare; Children's Home; Public Television; Society for the Blind; YMCA

Grants awarded to organizations located in Michigan.

Typical grant range: $4,000 to $30,000

303
Hudson-Webber Foundation
333 W. Fort Street, Suite 1310
Detroit, MI 48226
(313) 963-7777

Operating grants; cultural organizations; hospitals; community development; disabled; social welfare

Grants awarded to organizations located in the Detroit vicinity.

Typical grant range: $15,000 to $50,000

MICHIGAN

304
Hurst Foundation
105 E. Michigan Avenue
P.O. Box 449
Jackson, MI 49204
(517) 787-6503

Operating grants; social welfare; museums; community development; higher education; Television Station WKAR; United Way; Junior Achievement; Jackson Community Foundation; Historical Society; Speech and Hearing Clinic

Grants awarded to organizations located in Jackson County.

305
Jackson Community Foundation
230 W. Michigan Avenue
Jackson, MI 49201
(517) 787-1321

Operating grants; museums; social welfare; Girl Scouts; Junior Achievement

Grants awarded to organizations located in Jackson County.

Typical grant range: $1,500 to $25,000

306
Kalamazoo Foundation
151 S. Rose Street, Suite 332
Kalamazoo, MI 49007
(616) 381-4416

Operating grants; Arts Council of Greater Kalamazoo; Catholic Family Services; Greenwood Reformed Church; Family Institute (child care and educational programs); Specific Language Disability Center

Grants awarded to organizations located in Kalamazoo County.

307
Louis G. Kaufman Endowment Fund
MFC First National Bank
P.O. Box 580
Marquette, MI 49855
(906) 228-1244

Operating grants; social welfare; community development; youth organizations

Grants awarded to organizations located in Marquette.

Typical grant range: $1,000 to $9,000

308
Lyon Foundation, Inc.
1592 Redding
Birmingham, MI 48009

Operating grants; health organizations; hospitals; youth organizations; cultural organizations

Most grants awarded to organizations located in Michigan.

309
McGregor Fund
333 W. Fort Street, Suite 1380
Detroit, MI 48226
(313) 963-3495

Operating grants; youth organizations; social welfare; animal welfare; cultural organizations; community development; homeless; disabled

Grants awarded to organizations located in Detroit.

Typical grant range: $20,000 to $60,000

MICHIGAN

310
Frances Goll Mills Fund
Second National Bank of Saginaw
101 N. Washington Avenue
Saginaw, MI 48607
(517) 776-7582

Operating grants; social welfare; cultural organizations; hospitals

Grants awarded to organizations located in Saginaw County.

Typical grant range: $1,000 to $9,000

311
Morley Brothers Foundation
One Tuscola Street
P.O. Box 2485
Saginaw, MI 48605
(517) 753-3438

Operating grants; youth organizations; social welfare; cultural organizations

Grants awarded to organizations located in the Saginaw vicinity.

312
Muskegon County Community Foundation, Inc.
Community Foundation Building
425 W. Western Avenue
Muskegon, MI 49440
(616) 722-4538

Operating grants; cultural organizations; hospitals; health organizations; disabled; community development

Grants awarded to organizations located in Muskegon County.

Typical grant range: $2,000 to $25,000

313
Sage Foundation
10315 Grand River Road, Suite 204
Brighton, MI 48116

Operating grants; disabled; health organizations; hospitals; cultural organizations; youth organizations

Grants awarded to organizations located in Michigan.

Typical grant range: $2,500 to $50,000

314
Skillman Foundation
333 W. Fort Street, Suite 1350
Detroit, MI 48226
(313) 961-8850

Operating grants; child welfare; disabled; social welfare; all levels of education; public libraries; cultural organizations

Typical grant range: $25,000 to $150,000

315
A. Alfred Taubman Foundation
200 E. Long Lake Road
P.O. Box 200
Bloomfield Hills, MI 48303
(313) 258-6800

Operating grants; American Jewish Committee; Children of Alcoholics; Prostate Clinic; Black United Fund; Boy Scouts; United Negro College Fund; Detroit Symphony Orchestra; Gay Men's Health Crisis; Goodwill Industries; Juvenile Diabetes; National Abortion Rights; Salvation Army; Planned Parenthood; Michigan Cancer Foundation; Visiting Nurse Association; World Wildlife Association; United Way

Grants awarded to organizations located in Michigan.

Typical grant range: $250 to $10,000

316
Taubman Charitable Foundation
200 E. Long Lake Road
P.O. Box 200
Bloomfield Hills, MI 48303

Operating grants; higher education; minorities; cultural organizations

317
Weatherwax Foundation
618 N. Mechanic Street
P.O. Box 1111
Jackson, MI 49204
(517) 787-2117

Operating grants; Animal Protective Association; Cascades Humane Society; Culver Educational Foundation; First United Methodist Church; Hospice; Jackson Symphony Orchestra; Jackson Youth Center; Salvation Army; Urban Services; Boy Scouts of America

Grants awarded to organizations located in Jackson.

Typical grant range: $3,000 to $50,000

318
Whirlpool Foundation
400 Riverview Drive, Suite 410
Benton Harbor, MI 49022
(616) 923-5112

Operating grants; cultural organizations; social welfare; disabled; community development

Grants awarded to organizations located in areas of company operations.

Typical grant range: $1,000 to $20,000

319
Harvey Randall Wickes Foundation
Plaza North, Suite 472
4800 Fashion Square Blvd.
Saginaw, MI 48604
(517) 799-1850

Operating grants; performing arts; museums; youth organizations; community development; higher education

Grants awarded to organizations located in the Saginaw vicinity.

Typical grant range: $5,000 to $40,000

320
Wickson-Link Memorial Foundation
P.O. Box 3275
3023 Davenport Street
Saginaw, MI 48605
(517) 793-9830

Operating grants; Boys and Girls Club; Child Abuse and Neglect Council; City of Frankenmoth-Heritage Park; First Christian Church; Historical Society; Habitat for Humanity; Hospital Council Foundation; Saginaw General Hospital; Junior Achievement; Saginaw Art Museum; Saginaw Choral Society and Symphony Orchestra; Special Olympics; Saginaw Public Libraries; United Way; Visiting Nurses Association; Saginaw Valley State University Foundation

Grants awarded to organizations located in the Saginaw vicinity.

321
Lula C. Wilson Trust
c/o NBD Bank, N.A.
1116 W. Long Lake Road
Bloomfield Hills, MI 48013
(313) 645-7306

Operating grants; social welfare; disabled; women; community development; youth organizations; cultural organizations

322
Matilda R. Wilson Fund
100 Renaissance Center, 33rd Fl.
Detroit, MI 48243
(313) 259-7777

Operating grants; social welfare; youth organizations; disabled; cultural organizations

Typical grant range: $15,000 to $50,000

323
World Heritage Foundation
One Heritage Place, Suite 400
Southgate, MI 48195

Operating grants; Children's Hospital of Michigan; Detroit Zoological Society; YMCA; WTVS-Channel 56 Public TV; Southern Concerts; Boy Scouts/Girls Scouts; World Cup Soccer; Alzheimer's Care Notables; Leukemia Society of America; Salvation Army; Madonna College; Hospital of SE Michigan; World Medical Relief; Detroit Opera House; Food Bank; Family AIDS Network; American Heart Association

Grants awarded to organizations located in Michigan.

Typical grant range: $1,000 to $25,000

MINNESOTA

324
AHS Foundation
c/o First Trust, N.A.
P.O. Box 64704
St. Paul, MN 55164
(612) 291-5128

Operating grants; social welfare; environment; disabled; community development; cultural organizations

Typical grant range: $2,000 to $8,000

325
Athwin Foundation
4900 IDS Tower
80 South 8th Street
Minneapolis, MN 55402
(612) 340-3616

Operating grants; cultural organizations; community development; child welfare

Most grants awarded to organizations located in the Minneapolis-St. Paul vicinity.

Typical grant range: $2,000 to $25,000

326
Baker Foundation
4900 IDS Center
Minneapolis, MN 55402
(612) 332-7479

Operating grants; community development; youth organizations; environment; hospitals

Grants awarded to organizations located in Minnesota.

327
Otto Bremer Foundation
445 Minnesota Street, Suite 2000
St. Paul, MN 55101
(612) 227-8036

Operating grants; women; disabled; homeless; child welfare; minorities; community development; health organizations

Grants awarded to organizations located in areas of company operations (Bremer Bank).

Typical grant range: $2,000 to $20,000

MINNESOTA

328
Cargill Foundation
P.O. Box 5690
Minneapolis, MN 55440
(612) 472-6209

Operating grants; social welfare; environment; youth organizations; cultural organizations

Grants awarded to organizations located in the Minneapolis-St. Paul vicinity.

Typical grant range: $5,000 to $35,000

329
Cray Research Foundation
1440 Northland Drive
Mendota Heights, MN 55120
(612) 683-7379

Operating grants; educational institutions supporting science, engineering, and mathematics; higher education

Most grants awarded to organizations located in Minnesota.

Typical grant range: $1,500 to $25,000

330
Edwin W. and Catherine M. Davis Foundation
332 Minnesota Street, Suite 2100
St. Paul, MN 55101
(612) 228-0935

Operating grants; social welfare; youth organizations; cultural organizations

331
Dayton Hudson Foundation
777 Nicollet Mall
Minneapolis, MN 55402
(612) 370-6555

Operating grants; youth organizations; community development; cultural organizations; social welfare

Grants awarded to organizations located in areas of company operations.

Typical grant range: $5,000 to $80,000

332
Deluxe Corporation Foundation
P.O. Box 64399
St. Paul, MN 55164
(612) 483-7842

Operating grants; cultural organizations; social welfare; youth organizations

Grants awarded to organizations located in areas of company operations.

Typical grant range: $1,000 to $14,000

333
Doherty, Rumble & Butler Foundation
2800 Minnesota World Trade Center
30 E. Seventh Street
St. Paul, MN 55101
(612) 291-9333

Operating grants; cultural organizations; elderly; social welfare

Many grants awarded in the St. Paul vicinity.

Typical grant range: $500 to $2,500

334
Duluth-Superior Area Community Foundation
618 Missabe Building
227 W. First Street
Duluth, MN 55802
(218) 726-0232

Operating grants; museums; youth organizations; social welfare; child welfare; disabled; hospitals; Public Libraries; Food Banks

Typical grant range: $1,000 to $9,000

335
First Bank System Foundation
P.O. Box 522
Minneapolis, MN 55480

Operating grants; all levels of education; disabled; cultural organizations; community development; social welfare

Grants awarded to organizations located in areas of company operations.

Typical grant range: $1,000 to $8,000

MINNESOTA

336
General Mills Foundation
P.O. Box 1113
Minneapolis, MN 55440
(612) 540-7891

Operating grants; cultural organizations; disabled; higher education; secondary education; community development; youth organizations; minorities

Grants awarded to organizations located in areas of company operations, with an emphasis in Minneapolis.

Typical grant range: $3,000 to $25,000

337
Graco Foundation
P.O. Box 1441
Minneapolis, MN 55440
(612) 623-6684

Operating grants; disabled; youth organizations; community development; social welfare

Grants awarded to organizations located in areas of company operations.

Typical grant range: $1,000 to $5,000

338
Grand Metropolitan Food Sector Foundation
Mail Station 37X5
200 S. Sixth Street
Minneapolis, MN 55402
(612) 330-5434

Operating grants; youth organizations; cultural organizations; minorities

Grants awarded to organizations located in areas of company operations (Pillsbury Company).

Typical grant range: $1,000 to $20,000

339
Greystone Foundation
400 Baker Building
706 Second Avenue South
Minneapolis, MN 55402
(612) 332-2454

Operating grants; community development; animal welfare; health organizations; cultural organizations

Grants awarded to organizations located in Minnesota.

340
Mary Livingston Griggs and Mary Griggs Burke Foundation
1400 Norwest Center
55 E. Fifth Street
St. Paul, MN 55101
(612) 227-7683

Operating grants; social welfare; hospitals; cultural organizations

341
Honeywell Foundation
Honeywell Plaza
P.O. Box 524
Minneapolis, MN 55440
(612) 951-2368

Operating grants; social welfare; all levels of education; community development; youth organizations

Grants awarded to organizations located in areas of company operations, with an emphasis in Minneapolis.

Typical grant range: $1,000 to $25,000

342
International Multifoods Charitable Foundation
Multifoods Tower, Box 2942
Minneapolis, MN 55402
(612) 340-3410

Operating grants; performing arts; higher education; anticrime program; youth organizations

Typical grant range: $1,000 to $5,000

MINNESOTA

343
Jostens Foundation, Inc.
5501 Norman Center Drive
Minneapolis, MN 55437
(612) 830-8461

Operating grants; social welfare; minorities; youth organizations; disabled; all levels of education; cultural organizations

Most grants awarded to organizations located in Minnesota.

Typical grant range: $1,000 to $7,500

344
MAHADH Foundation
287 Central Avenue
Bayport, MN 55003
(612) 439-1557

Operating grants; social welfare; performing arts; museums; health organizations; youth organizations; disabled

345
McKnight Foundation
600 TCF Tower
121 S. Eighth Street
Minneapolis, MN 55402
(612) 333-4220

Operating grants; social welfare; cultural organizations; community development; disabled; youth organizations

Grants awarded to organizations located in Minnesota.

Typical grant range: $20,000 to $200,000

346
Medtronic Foundation
7000 Central Avenue, N.E.
Minneapolis, MN 55432
(612) 574-3024

Operating grants; elderly; health organizations; cultural organizations; social welfare; community development

Grants awarded to organizations located in areas of company operations.

Typical grant range: $3,000 to $15,000

347
Minneapolis Foundation
A200 Foshay Tower
821 Marquette Avenue South
Minneapolis, MN 55402
(612) 339-7343

Operating grants; community development; social welfare; minorities; cultural organizations; disabled

Grants awarded to organizations located in the Minneapolis-St. Paul vicinity.

Typical grant range: $1,000 to $25,000

348
Minnesota Mining and Manufacturing Foundation, Inc.
3 M Center Building 591-30-02
St. Paul, MN 55144

Operating grants; youth organizations; community development; cultural organizations; disabled; health organizations

Grants awarded to organizations located in areas of company operations.

Typical grant range: $500 to $20,000

349
Myers Foundation, Inc.
1507 Edgcumbe Road
St. Paul, MN 55116

Operating grants; social welfare; higher education; cultural organizations; Public Television/Public Radio; Churches; Opera/Orchestral Association; American Red Cross; Children's Home Society; Family Service; Food Bank; United Way; Children's Hospital; Humane Society; Institute of Art; Science Museum

Many grants awarded in the St. Paul and the Minneapolis vicinity.

Most grants awarded to preselected organizations.

Typical grant range: $500 to $2,500

MINNESOTA

350
Northwestern National Life Foundation
20 Washington Ave. South
Minneapolis, MN 55401
(612) 342-7443

Operating grants; social welfare; child welfare; disabled; women; cultural organizations; hospitals; health organizations

Grants awarded to organizations located in the Minneapolis vicinity.

351
Alice M. O'Brien Foundation
324 Forest
Mahtomedi, MN 55115
(612) 426-2143

Operating grants; social welfare; cultural organizations

Grants awarded to organizations located in Minnesota.

Typical grant range: $1,000 to $8,000

352
Casey Albert T. O'Neil Foundation
c/o First Trust, N.A.
P.O. Box 64704
St. Paul, MN 55164
(612) 291-5139

Operating grants; disabled; child welfare; youth organizations; health organizations

Grants awarded to organizations located in the St. Paul vicinity.

Typical grant range: $1,500 to $15,000

353
Ordean Foundation
501 Ordean Building
424 W. Superior Street
Duluth, MN 55802
(218) 726-4785

Operating grants; health organizations; youth organizations; social welfare; disabled; women

Typical grant range: $500 to $25,000

354
Rodman Foundation
2100 First National Bank Bldg.
St. Paul, MN 55101
(612) 228-0935

Operating grants; higher education; Children's Theater Company; Nature Center; Freshwater Foundation/World Wildlife Fund; Arboretum; Planned Parenthood; Children's Home; United Way; University Preparatory Academy; YMCA; Children's Fund; Hospital for Children; Public Television; Union Gospel Mission

Grants awarded to organizations located in Minnesota.

Typical grant range: $500 to $2,000

355
Harold J. and Marie O'Brien Slawik Foundation
1951 University Avenue West
St. Paul, MN 55104
(612) 645-8111

Operating grants; social welfare; child welfare; community development; Christian organizations

Grants awarded to organizations located in Ramsey County.

356
St. Croix Foundation
c/o First Trust, N.A.
P.O. Box 64367
St. Paul, MN 55164
(612) 244-0939

Operating grants; health organizations; hospitals; cultural organizations; social welfare; youth organizations; Churches

357
James R. Thorpe Foundation
8085 Wayzata Blvd.
Minneapolis, MN 55426
(612) 545-1111

Operating grants; youth organizations; elderly; health organizations; cultural organizations; social welfare; disabled; AIDS

Grants awarded to organizations located in the Minneapolis vicinity.

Typical grant range: $1,500 to $5,000

358
Tozer Foundation, Inc.
104 N. Main Street
Stillwater, MN 55082
(612) 439-4143

Operating grants; cultural organizations; community development; disabled; Courage Center; YWCA; Family Services; Historical Society

Grants awarded to organizations located in Minnesota.

MISSISSIPPI

359
Deposit Guaranty Foundation
One Deposit Guaranty Plaza
P.O. Box 730
Jackson, MS 39205

Operating grants; community development; social welfare; hospitals; cultural organizations

Grants awarded to organizations located in Mississippi.

360
First Mississippi Corporation Foundation, Inc.
700 North Street
P.O. Box 1249
Jackson, MS 39215
(601) 948-7550

Operating grants; community development; youth organizations

Grants awarded to organizations located in areas of company operations.

361
Phil Hardin Foundation
c/o Citizens National Bank
P.O. Box 911
Meridian, MS 39302
(601) 483-4282

Operating grants; higher education; minorities

Most grants awarded to organizations located in Mississippi.

Typical grant range: $5,000 to $40,000

MISSOURI

362
H & R Block Foundation
4410 Main Street
Kansas City, MO 64111
(816) 753-6900

Operating grants; cultural organizations; community development; health organizations; social welfare; AIDS

Grants awarded to organizations located in the Kansas City vicinity.

MISSOURI

363
Brown Group, Inc. Charitable Trust
8400 Maryland Avenue
Clayton, MO 63105
(314) 854-4093

Operating grants; social welfare; community development; cultural organizations; youth organizations; hospitals

Grants awarded to organizations located in areas of company operations, with an emphasis in St. Louis.

Typical grant range: $100 to $12,000

364
CPI Corporation Philanthropic Trust
1706 Washington Avenue
St. Louis, MO 63103
(314) 231-1575

Operating grants; social welfare; child welfare; cultural organizations; Jewish organizations

Grants awarded to organizations located in areas of company operations.

Typical grant range: $1,000 to $7,000

365
Milton W. Feld Charitable Trust
2345 Grand Avenue, Suite 2800
Kansas City, MO 64108
(816) 292-2124

Operating grants; hospitals; child welfare; social welfare; AIDS; Jewish organizations

Most grants awarded to organizations located in Kansas City and St. Louis.

Typical grant range: $1,000 to $11,000

366
Hallmark Corporate Foundation
P.O. Box 419580, Mail Drop 323
Kansas City, MO 64141

Operating grants; cultural organizations; community development; social welfare

Typical grant range: $2,000 to $25,000

367
Laclede Gas Charitable Trust
720 Olive Street, Room 1525
St. Louis, MO 63101
(314) 342-0859

Operating grants; cultural organizations; youth organizations; elderly; health organizations; child welfare; social welfare; animal welfare; community development; disabled

Grants awarded to organizations located in areas of company operations.

Typical grant range: $3,000 to $20,000

368
R.A. Long Foundation
600 Plaza West Building
4600 Madison Avenue
Kansas City, MO 64112
(816) 561-4600

Operating grants; child welfare; youth organizations; recreation; disabled

Grants awarded to organizations located in the Kansas City vicinity.

Typical grant range: $2,000 to $7,000

369
McGee Foundation
4900 Main Street, Suite 717
Kansas City, MO 64112
(816) 931-1515

Operating grants; Truman Medical Center; Children's Center for the Visually Impaired; Learning Exchange; Kansas City Hospice; Donnelly College; Avila College

Grants awarded to organizations located in the Kansas City vicinity.

370
Finis M. Moss Charitable Trust
108 West Walnut
P.O. Box J
Nevada, MO 64772
(417) 667-5076

Operating grants; Vernon County Humane Society; Children's Mercy Hospital; Shrine Club Crippled Children's Transportation Fund; Community Food Pantry; Moss Preschool and Child Care; Salvation Army; HEADSTART; Vernon County Ambulance District

Grants awarded to organizations located in Nevada, Missouri.

371
PET Incorporated Community Support Foundation
400 S. Fourth Street
St. Louis, MO 63102
(314) 621-5400

Operating grants; social welfare; cultural organizations; youth organizations; community development

Grants awarded to organizations located in Missouri, with an emphasis in St. Louis.

Typical grant range: $2,000 to $15,000

372
Herman T. and Phenie R. Pott Foundation
1034 S. Brentwood, Suite 1480
St. Louis, MO 63117
(314) 725-8477

Operating grants; disabled; social welfare; elderly; youth organizations

Most grants awarded to organizations located in the St. Louis vicinity.

373
Pulitzer Publishing Company Foundation
900 N. Tucker Blvd.
St. Louis, MO 63101
(314) 622-7000

Operating grants; cultural organizations; minorities; youth organizations; social welfare; child welfare

Most grants awarded to organizations located in the St. Louis vicinity.

Typical grant range: $2,500 to $10,000

374
Roy W. Slusher Charitable Foundation
P.O. Box 10327
Springfield, MO 65808
(417) 882-9090

Operating grants; Ozark Christian Counseling

Grants awarded to organizations located in Missouri.

Typical grant range: $500 to $20,000

375
John W. and Effie E. Speas Memorial Trust
c/o Boatmen's First National Bank of Kansas City
14 W. Tenth Street
Kansas City, MO 64183
(816) 691-7481

Operating grants; child welfare; disabled; elderly

Most grants awarded to organizations located in the Kansas City vicinity.

Typical grant range: $5,000 to $80,000

376
Victor E. Speas Foundation
Boatmen's First National Bank of
Kansas City
14 W. Tenth Street
Kansas City, MO 64183
(816) 691-7481

Operating grants; disabled; youth organizations; elderly; health organizations; AIDS

Grants awarded to organizations located in the Kansas City vicinity.

377
St. Louis Community Foundation
818 Olive Street, Suite 935
St. Louis, MO 63101
(314) 241-2703

Operating grants; environment; disabled; elderly; social welfare; recreation; cultural organizations; community development

Grants awarded to organizations located in the St. Louis vicinity.

Typical grant range: $500 to $9,000

378
Norman J. Stupp Foundation
c/o Commerce Bank of St. Louis, N.A.
8000 Forsyth, Suite 1305
St. Louis, MO 63105
(314) 746-8577

Operating grants; youth organizations; social welfare; health organizations; hospitals

Most grants awarded to organizations located in the St. Louis vicinity.

Typical grant range: $3,000 to $30,000

379
Courtney S. Turner Charitable Trust
c/o Boatmen's First National Bank of
Kansas City
P.O. Box 419038
Kansas City, MO 64183
(816) 691-7481

Operating grants; higher education; performing arts

Typical grant range: $3,000 to $80,000

380
Union Electric Company Charitable Trust
1901 Chouteau Street
P.O. Box 149
St. Louis, MO 63166
(314) 621-3222

Operating grants; community development; disabled; social welfare; hospitals; cultural organizations

Grants awarded to organizations located in areas of company operations.

Typical grant range: $5,000 to $35,000

381
Webb Foundation
7711 Carondelet Avenue, Suite 810
St. Louis, MO 63105
(314) 862-6220

Operating grants; disabled; health organizations; hospitals; social welfare; child welfare

MONTANA

382
Dufresne Foundation
P.O. Box 1484
Great Falls, MT 59403
(406) 452-9414

Operating grants; social welfare; cultural organizations; child welfare; health organizations; youth organizations

Grants awarded to organizations located in Montana.

NEBRASKA

383
Alan and Marcia Baer Foundation
5015 Underwood Avenue
Omaha, NE 68132
(402) 556-0464

Operating grants; health organizations; cultural organizations

Grants awarded to organizations located in Omaha.

384
Theodore G. Baldwin Foundation
P.O. Box 922
Kearney, NE 68848
(308) 234-9889

Operating grants; cultural organizations

Grants awarded to organizations located in Nebraska.

385
Imperial Foundation
852 NBC Center
Lincoln, NE 68508
(402) 475-4204

Operating grants; museums; performing arts; youth organizations; Churches

Grants awarded to organizations located in Nebraska.

Small value grants.

386
Lied Foundation Trust
10050 Regency Circle, Suite 200
Omaha, NE 68114

Operating grants; higher education; Institute for Contemporary Art; Discover Museum; Salvation Army; Boys and Girls Club; St. Vincent's Dining Room; Churches; Dance Theatre

Typical grant range: $150,000 to $600,000

387
Stuart Foundation
825 NBC Center
Lincoln, NE 68508
(402) 475-4204

Operating grants; Fellowship of Christian Athletes; Nebraska Game and Parks Foundation; YMCA

Typical grant range: $300 to $2,000

NEVADA

388
First Interstate Bank of Nevada Foundation
P.O. Box 98588
Las Vegas, NV 89193
(702) 791-6462

Operating grants; cultural organizations; social welfare; community development

Grants awarded to organizations located in Nevada.

Typical grant range: $5,000 to $12,000

389
Gabelli Foundation, Inc.
c/o Avansino, Melarkey & Knobel
165 W. Liberty Street
Reno, NV 89501

Operating grants; secondary education; hospitals; Museum of Art; Winston Churchill Foundation

Most grants awarded to organizations located in Reno.

Typical grant range: $1,000 to $20,000

390
Conrad N. Hilton Foundation
100 W. Liberty Street, Suite 840
Reno, NV 89501
(702) 323-4221

Operating grants; drug abuse; health organizations; higher education; Catholic organizations

Typical grant range: $5,000 to $75,000

NEW HAMPSHIRE

391
Chatam, Inc.
Liberty Lane
Hampton, NH 03842
(603) 926-5911

Operating grants; social welfare; performing arts; museums; zoos; animal welfare; higher education

Typical grant range: $2,000 to $35,000

392
Agnes M. Lindsay Trust
95 Market Street
Manchester, NH 03101
(603) 669-4140

Operating grants; disabled; child welfare; health organizations; social welfare; higher education; youth organizations

Typical grant range: $1,500 to $7,500

393
New Hampshire Ball Bearings, Inc. Foundation
c/o New Hampshire Ball Bearings, Inc.
U.S. Route 202 South
Peterborough, NH 03458

Operating grants; cultural organizations; recreation; social welfare; community development

Grants awarded to organizations located in areas of company operations.

Typical grant range: $500 to $3,000

NEW JERSEY

394
AlliedSignal Foundation
P.O. Box 2245
Morristown, NJ 07962
(201) 455-5877

Operating grants; community development; health organizations; elderly; disabled; youth organizations; cultural organizations

Grants awarded to organizations located in areas of company operations.

Typical grant range: $1,000 to $12,000

395
Johnson & Johnson Family of Companies Contribution Fund
One Johnson & Johnson Plaza
New Brunswick, NJ 08933
(201) 524-3255

Operating grants; health organizations; hospitals; cultural organizations; elderly

Grants awarded to organizations located in areas of company operations.

Typical grant range: $5,000 to $30,000

396
Maneely Fund, Inc.
900 Haddon Avenue, Suite 432
Collingswood, NJ 08108
(609) 854-5400

Operating grants; St. Christopher's Church; St. Joseph's Villa

397
Schering-Plough Foundation, Inc.
One Giralda Farms
P.O. Box 1000
Madison, NJ 07940
(201) 822-7412

Operating grants; health organizations; hospitals; cultural organizations

Grants awarded to organizations located in areas of company operations.

Typical grant range: $10,000 to $25,000

NEW JERSEY

398
Schultz Foundation
825 Bloomfield Avenue, Suite 105
Verona, NJ 07044

Operating grants; West Essex Hospice; Memorial Sloan-Kettering Cancer Center; National Council on Alcoholism and Drug Dependence; New Jersey Historical Society

399
Florence and John Schumann Foundation
33 Park Street
Montclair, NJ 07042
(201) 783-6660

Operating grants; environment; community development

Typical grant range: $15,000 to $50,000

400
Schumann Fund for New Jersey, Inc.
33 Park Street
Montclair, NJ 07042
(201) 509-9883

Operating grants; homeless; child welfare; social welfare

Grants awarded to organizations located in New Jersey.

Typical grant range: $10,000 to $50,000

401
Arnold A. Schwartz Foundation
c/o Kunzman, Coley, Yospin & Bernstein
15 Mountain Blvd.
Warren, NJ 07060
(908) 757-7927

Operating grants; Rescue Squad; Edison Sheltered Workshop; United Family and Childrens Society

Typical grant range: $1,000 to $8,000

402
Tomlinson Family Foundation, Inc.
P.O. Box 590
Morristown, NJ 07963

Operating grants; Jersey's Battered Women's Service; Time-Out Adult Care Center; Historic Speedwell; Market Street Mission; Recording for the Blind; Summit Speech School

Grants awarded to organizations located in New Jersey.

403
Turrell Fund
21 Van Vleck Street
Montclair, NJ 07042
(201) 783-9358

Operating grants; youth organizations; disabled; child welfare; social welfare; recreation

Most grants awarded to organizations located in New Jersey.

Typical grant range: $5,000 to $35,000

404
Warner-Lambert Charitable Foundation
201 Tabor Road
Morris Plains, NJ 07950
(201) 540-3652

Operating grants; community development; youth organizations; social welfare; hospitals

Grants awarded to organizations located in areas of company operations.

Typical grant range: $5,000 to $30,000

405
Westfield Foundation
301 North Ave. West
P.O. Box 2295
Westfield, NJ 07091
(908) 233-9787

Operating grants; child welfare; disabled; community development

Grants awarded to organizations located in Westfield.

NEW YORK

406
Achelis Foundation
c/o Morris & McVeigh
767 Third Avenue
New York, NY 10017
(212) 418-0588

Operating grants; disabled; cultural organizations; homeless; social welfare; health organizations; youth organizations; recreation; community development

Grants awarded to organizations located in New York City.

Typical grant range: $10,000 to $25,000

407
American Conservation Association
30 Rockefeller Plaza, Suite 5402
New York, NY 10112
(212) 649-5822

Operating grants; environment; land conservation

Grants awarded throughout the United States.

Typical grant range: $15,000 to $60,000

408
AT&T Foundation
1301 Avenue of the Americas, Suite 3100
New York, NY 10019
(212) 841-4747

Operating grants; cultural organizations; disabled; youth organizations; minorities; women; health organizations; AIDS

Grants awarded to organizations located in areas of company operations.

Typical grant range: $5,000 to $40,000

409
Bodman Foundation
c/o Morris & McVeigh
767 Third Avenue, 22nd Floor
New York, NY 10017
(212) 418-0500

Operating grants; social welfare; community development; elderly; disabled; youth organizations

Grants awarded to organizations located in the New York City vicinity.

Typical grant range: $15,000 to $50,000

410
BT Foundation
280 Park Ave.
New York, NY 10017
(212) 454-3086

Operating grants; social welfare; minorities; higher education; performing arts; museums; disabled; community development

Most grants awarded to organizations located in New York City.

Typical grant range: $10,000 to $20,000

411
Buffalo Foundation
1601 Main-Seneca Building
237 Main Street
Buffalo, NY 14203
(716) 852-2857

Operating grants; social welfare; animal welfare; cultural organizations; disabled; youth organizations; community development; St. Philip's Community Center

Grants awarded to organizations located in Erie County.

Typical grant range: $1,000 to $15,000

412
Louis Calder Foundation
230 Park Avenue, Room 1530
New York, NY 10169
(212) 687-1680

Operating grants; minorities; social welfare; health organizations; youth organizations

Grants awarded to organizations located in New York City.

Typical grant range: $10,000 to $40,000

413
Chase Manhattan Foundation
The Chase Manhattan Bank, N.A.
Two Chase Manhattan Plaza
New York, NY 10081
(212) 552-8205

Operating grants; social welfare; child welfare; minorities; youth organizations; community development; hospitals; health organizations

Typical grant range: $2,000 to $8,000

414
Clark Foundation
30 Wall Street
New York, NY 10005
(212) 269-1833

Operating grants; disabled; child welfare; environment; minorities; health organizations; AIDS

Typical grant range: $15,000 to $80,000

415
Peter C. Cornell Trust
c/o Fiduciary Services, Inc.
4476 Main Street, Suite 206
Snyder, NY 14226
(716) 839-3005

Operating grants; social welfare; health organizations

Typical grant range: $2,000 to $9,000

416
Cowles Charitable Trust
630 Fifth Avenue, Suite 1612
New York, NY 10111
(212) 765-6262

Operating grants; cultural organizations; community development; child welfare; health organizations; AIDS

Typical grant range: $3,000 to $25,000

417
Aaron Diamond Foundation, Inc.
1270 Avenue of the Americas, Suite 2624
New York, NY 10020
(212) 757-7680

Operating grants; cultural organizations; women; health organizations; hospitals; minorities; social welfare; Public Library; AIDS

Grants awarded to organizations located in New York City.

Typical grant range: $15,000 to $60,000

418
Dorr Foundation
P.O. Box 281
Bedford, NY 10506
(914) 234-3573

Operating grants; environment; Botanical Gardens

419
Gebbie Foundation, Inc.
Hotel Jamestown Building, Suite 308
P.O. Box 1277
Jamestown, NY 14702
(716) 487-1062

Operating grants; Children's Village; Chautauqua Lake Association; Corry Memorial Hospital

Most grants awarded to organizations located in Chautauqua County.

Typical grant range: $2,000 to $35,000

NEW YORK

420
Rosamond Gifford Charitable Corporation
731 James Street, Room 404
Syracuse, NY 13203
(315) 474-2489

Operating grants; elderly; hospitals; child welfare; community development; cultural organizations

Grants awarded to organizations located in the Syracuse vicinity.

421
Gleason Memorial Fund, Inc.
1000 University Avenue
Rochester, NY 14692
(716) 272-6005

Operating grants; social welfare; cultural organizations; youth organizations

Grants awarded to organizations located in Rochester.

Typical grant range: $4,000 to $45,000

422
Hagedorn Fund
c/o Chemical Bank
270 Park Avenue
New York, NY 10017

Operating grants; health organizations; elderly; youth organizations; social welfare; AIDS; Churches

Most grants awarded to organizations located in the New York City vicinity.

Typical grant range: $3,000 to $20,000

423
Mary W. Harriman Foundation
63 Wall Street, 23rd Floor
New York, NY 10005
(212) 493-8182

Operating grants; cultural organizations; health organizations; social welfare; youth organizations

424
Hearst Foundation, Inc.
888 Seventh Avenue, 45th Floor
New York, NY 10106
(212) 586-5404

Operating grants; performing arts; museums; animal welfare; disabled; social welfare; minorities

Typical grant range: $10,000 to $40,000

425
Stewart W. & Willma C. Hoyt Foundation
105-107 Court Street, Suite 400
Binghamton, NY 13901
(607) 722-6706

Operating grants; social welfare; cultural organizations; health organizations; AIDS

Grants awarded to organizations located in Broome County.

Typical grant range: $5,000 to $25,000

426
Christian A. Johnson Endeavor Foundation
1060 Park Avenue
New York, NY 10128
(212) 534-6620

Operating grants; cultural organizations; all levels of education

Typical grant range: $10,000 to $35,000

427
Daisy Marquis Jones Foundation
620 Granite Building
130 E. Main Street
Rochester, NY 14604
(716) 263-3331

Operating grants; health organizations; disabled; youth organizations; women; elderly

Grants awarded to organizations located in Monroe and Yates Counties.

Typical grant range: $3,000 to $20,000

NEW YORK

428
Joy Family Foundation
107-111 Goundry Street
North Tonawanda, NY 14120
(716) 692-6665

Operating grants; social welfare; Sisters of St. Francis; Buffalo Philharmonic Orchestra Society

Typical grant range: $1,500 to $20,000

429
Eugene M. Lang Foundation
155 E. 38th Street
New York, NY 10016
(212) 687-4741

Operating grants; social welfare; cultural organizations; minorities

Typical grant range: $2,000 to $20,000

430
James A. Macdonald Foundation
One N. Broadway
White Plains, NY 10601
(914) 428-9305

Operating grants; health organizations; child welfare; youth organizations; Churches

431
McGraw-Hill Foundation, Inc.
1221 Avenue of the Americas, Suite 2917
New York, NY 10020
(212) 512-6113

Operating grants; disabled; cultural organizations; social welfare; health organizations

Grants awarded to organizations located in areas of company operations.

Typical grant range: $500 to $6,000

432
MCJ Foundation
375 Park Avenue, Suite 301
New York, NY 10152
(212) 735-1125

Operating grants; child welfare; youth organizations; community development; cultural organizations

Typical grant range: $500 to $20,000

433
Merrill Lynch & Company Foundation, Inc.
South Tower, 6th Floor
World Financial Center
New York, NY 10080
(212) 236-4319

Operating grants; cultural organizations; social welfare; disabled; health organizations; AIDS

Typical grant range: $3,000 to $40,000

434
Stanley W. Metcalf Foundation, Inc.
120 Genesee Street, Suite 503
Auburn, NY 13021
(315) 253-9321

Operating grants; social welfare; youth organizations; Churches

Grants awarded to organizations located in Cayuga County.

435
J. P. Morgan Charitable Trust
60 Wall Street, 46th Floor
New York, NY 10260
(212) 648-9673

Operating grants; social welfare; child welfare; health organizations; hospitals; AIDS

Grants awarded to organizations located in the New York City vicinity.

Typical grant range: $5,000 to $30,000

NEW YORK

436
Henry and Lucy Moses Fund, Inc.
c/o Moses & Singer
1301 Avenue of the Americas
New York, NY 10019
(212) 554-7800

Operating grants; social welfare; disabled; minorities; cultural organizations; environment; AIDS

Most grants awarded to organizations located in the New York City vicinity.

Typical grant range: $3,000 to $12,000

437
New Street Foundation, Inc.
450 Lexington Avenue, 14th Floor
New York, NY 10017
(212) 450-7926

Operating grants; health organizations; disabled; minorities; social welfare

Most grants awarded to organizations located in the New York City vicinity.

Typical grant range: $10,000 to $40,000

438
New York Life Foundation
51 Madison Avenue
New York, NY 10010
(212) 576-7341

Operating grants; minorities; performing arts; museums; social welfare; AIDS

Typical grant range: $1,000 to $20,000

439
Jane W. Nuhn Charitable Trust
c/o Van DeWater & Van DeWater
P.O. Box 112
Poughkeepsie, NY 12602
(914) 452-5900

Operating grants; Dutchess County Arts Fund

Most grants awarded to organizations located in the Poughkeepsie vicinity.

Typical grant range: $2,000 to $30,000

440
Palisades Educational Foundation, Inc.
c/o Gibney, Anthony & Flaherty
665 Fifth Avenue, 2nd Floor
New York, NY 10022

Operating grants; Coalition for the Homeless

Typical grant range: $2,000 to $30,000

441
Pfizer Foundation, Inc.
Last minute update: this foundation has temporarily suspended their grant program

442
Louis and Harold Price Foundation, Inc.
654 Madison Avenue, Suite 2005
New York, NY 10021
(212) 753-0240

Operating grants; social welfare; cultural organizations; disabled; youth organizations; health organizations; Jewish organizations

Typical grant range: $200 to $5,000

443
Prospect Hill Foundation, Inc.
420 Lexington Avenue, Suite 3020
New York, NY 10170
(212) 370-1144

Operating grants; Jewish Home for the Elderly; National Audubon Society; Symphony Orchestra; Samuel Waxman Cancer Research Foundation

Typical grant range: $3,000 to $30,000

NEW YORK

444
Paul Rapoport Foundation, Inc.
220 E. 60th Street, Suite 14K
New York, NY 10022
(212) 888-6578

Operating grants; social welfare; community development; AIDS

Grants awarded to organizations located in New York City.

Typical grant range: $1,000 to $20,000

445
Gerald and May Ellen Ritter Memorial Fund
c/o Proskauer Rose Goetz & Mendelsohn
1585 Broadway, 25th Floor
New York, NY 10036

Operating grants; social welfare; cultural organizations; youth organizations; Jewish organizations

Grants awarded to organizations located in the New York City vicinity.

Typical grant range: $1,000 to $35,000

446
Helena Rubinstein Foundation, Inc.
405 Lexington Avenue
New York, NY 10174
(212) 986-0806

Operating grants; social welfare; youth organizations; disabled; women; child welfare

Grants awarded to organizations located in New York City.

Typical grant range: $3,000 to $20,000

447
Scherman Foundation, Inc.
315 West 57th Street, Suite 204
New York, NY 10019
(212) 489-7143

Operating grants; environment; social welfare; homeless; health organizations; cultural organizations; AIDS

Grants awarded to organizations located in New York City.

Typical grant range: $10,000 to $30,000

448
Shubert Foundation, Inc.
234 West 44th Street
New York, NY 10036
(212) 944-3777

Operating grants; performing arts; New York City Ballet

Typical grant range: $10,000 to $45,000

449
Sister Fund
1255 Fifth Ave., Suite C-2
New York, NY 10029
(212) 722-7606

Operating grants; women; social welfare; youth organizations; minorities; AIDS

Typical grant range: $5,000 to $35,000

450
Valentine Perry Snyder Fund
c/o Morgan Guaranty Trust Co. of New York
60 Wall Street
New York, NY 10260
(212) 648-9664

Operating grants; Council of Senior Centers and Services; Queens Child Guidance Center; Lenox Hill Neighborhood Association; Columbia University School of Nursing; Project Reach Youth; Brooklyn Bureau of Commercial Services

Grants awarded to organizations located in New York City.

451
Sony Corporation of America Foundation, Inc.
Nine W. 57th Street
New York, NY 10019
(212) 418-9404

Operating grants; cultural organizations; health organizations; hospitals; community development; youth organizations

Typical grant range: $500 to $50,000

452
Seth Sprague Educational and Charitable Foundation
c/o U.S. Trust Co. of New York
114 West 47th Street
New York, NY 10036
(212) 852-3683

Operating grants; cultural organizations; child welfare; youth organizations; health organizations; social welfare

Typical grant range: $2,000 to $5,000

453
United States Trust Company of New York Foundation
U.S. Trust Company of New York
114 W. 47th Street
New York, NY 10036
(212) 852-1000

Operating grants; cultural organizations; community development; health organizations

Most grants awarded to organizations located in the New York City vicinity.

Typical grant range: $4,000 to $10,000

454
van Ameringen Foundation, Inc.
509 Madison Avenue
New York, NY 10022
(212) 758-6221

Operating grants; mental health; social welfare; child welfare; hospitals; youth organizations

Typical grant range: $20,000 to $50,000

455
Louis A. Wehle Foundation
445 St. Paul Street
Rochester, NY 14605

Operating grants; social welfare; cultural organizations; community development

Grants awarded to organizations located in the Rochester vicinity.

Typical grant range: $1,000 to $4,000

456
Ralph Wilkens Foundation
222 Groton Avenue
Cortland, NY 13045
(607) 756-7548

Operating grants; Cortland Youth Bureau; Upstate Home for Children; Family Counseling Services; Cortland County Historical Society; Rural Health and Safety Council; YWCA

Grants awarded to organizations located in Cortland County.

Typical grant range: $500 to $7,000

457
Marie C. and Joseph C. Wilson Foundation
160 Allens Creek Road
Rochester, NY 14618
(716) 461-4699

Operating grants; social welfare; health organizations; cultural organizations; youth organizations

Grants awarded to organizations located in Rochester.

Typical grant range: $3,000 to $20,000

NORTH CAROLINA

458
Mary Reynolds Babcock Foundation, Inc.
102 Reynolda Village
Winston-Salem, NC 27106
(910) 748-9222

Operating grants; child welfare; women; social welfare; homeless; environment; cultural organizations

Most grants awarded to organizations located in North Carolina.

Typical grant range: $3,000 to $50,000

459
Belk Foundation
2801 W. Tyvola Road
Charlotte, NC 28217
(704) 357-1000

Operating grants; youth organizations; social welfare; environment; cultural organizations; hospitals; health organizations

Typical grant range: $2,000 to $20,000

460
Kathleen Price and Joseph M. Bryan Family Foundation
One N. Pointe, Suite 170
3101 N. Elm Street
Greensboro, NC 27408
(910) 288-5455

Operating grants; social welfare; cultural organizations; youth organizations; disabled; AIDS

Grants awarded to organizations located in North Carolina.

Typical grant range: $5,000 to $35,000

461
Cemala Foundation, Inc.
122 N. Elm Street, Suite 816
Greensboro, NC 27401
(910) 274-3541

Operating grants; Salvation Army; Greensboro Urban Ministry; Shepherd Center of Greensboro; North Carolina Children's Home Society; Greensboro Business Centre; University of North Carolina Center for Public TV; University of North Carolina Education Center; Greensboro Opera Company; North Carolina Literacy Association; Black Child Development; Arthritis Foundation; American Heart Association; Hospice at Greensboro; Zoological Society; Greensboro Crimestoppers; National Council of Christian and Jews

Grants awarded to organizations located in Guilford County.

Typical grant range: $1,500 to $8,000

462
Community Foundation of Henderson County, Inc.
4th Avenue and Main Street
P.O. Box 1108
Hendersonville, NC 28793
(704) 697-6224

Operating grants; homeless; social welfare

Grants awarded to organizations located in Henderson County.

Typical grant range: $250 to $5,000

463
Duke Endowment
100 N. Tryon Street, Suite 3500
Charlotte, NC 28202
(704) 376-0291

Operating grants; child welfare; youth organizations; elderly; hospitals; higher education

464
A.E. Finley Foundation, Inc.
P.O. Box 27785
Raleigh, NC 27611
(919) 782-0565

Operating grants; youth organizations; social welfare

Grants awarded to organizations located in North Carolina.

465
Glaxo Foundation
Five Moore Drive
Research Triangle Park, NC 27709
(919) 248-2140

Operating grants; all levels of education; health organizations

Grants awarded to organizations located in North Carolina.

Typical grant range: $20,000 to $100,000

466
Kayser-Roth Hosiery Charitable Foundation
4905 Koger Blvd.
Greensboro, NC 27407

Operating grants; Junior League of Greensboro; Food Bank; Penbrook State College

Grants awarded to organizations located in North Carolina.

Typical grant range: $2,000 to $10,000

467
Kate B. Reynolds Charitable Trust
128 Reynolda Village
Winston-Salem, NC 27106
(910) 723-1456

Operating grants; child welfare; social welfare; health organizations; homeless; elderly; AIDS

Grants awarded to organizations located in North Carolina.

Typical grant range: $25,000 to $75,000

468
Z. Smith Reynolds Foundation, Inc.
101 Reynolda Village
Winston-Salem, NC 27106
(910) 725-7541

Operating grants; minorities; women; community development; environment; cultural organizations; youth; Affordable Housing Coalition; Clean Water Fund; Greensboro Chinese Association; Wake Forest University; Eastern North Carolina Poverty Committee

Grants awarded to organizations located in North Carolina.

Typical grant range: $15,000 to $30,000

469
Wachovia Foundation Inc.
Wachovia Bank & Trust Co., N.A.
P.O. Box 3099
Winston-Salem, NC 27150

Operating grants; cultural organizations; health organizations; social welfare; child welfare

Grants awarded to organizations located in North Carolina, with an emphasis in communities with a Wachovia Bank branch.

Typical grant range: $3,000 to $30,000

NORTH DAKOTA

470
Tom and Frances Leach Foundation, Inc.
P.O. Box 1136
Bismarck, ND 58502
(701) 255-0479

Operating grants; youth organizations; social welfare; disabled; cultural organizations; health organizations

Grants awarded to organizations located in North Dakota.

Typical grant range: $1,500 to $9,000

471
North Dakota Community Foundation
P.O. Box 387
Bismarck, ND 58502
(701) 222-8349

Operating grants; elderly; social welfare; cultural organizations; health organizations; youth organizations

Grants awarded to organizations located in North Dakota.

Typical grant range: $250 to $2,000

472
Alex Stern Family Foundation
Bill Stern Building, Suite 205
609-1/2 First Avenue North
Fargo, ND 58102

Operating grants; child welfare; youth organizations; disabled; community development

OHIO

473
William H. Albers Foundation, Inc.
P.O. Box 58360
Cincinnati, OH 45258

Operating grants; disabled; cultural organizations; youth organizations; higher education

Most grants awarded to organizations located in Cincinnati.

Typical grant range: $1,000 to $7,000

474
American Financial Corporation Foundation
Last minute update: this foundation has been terminated.

475
Elsie and Harry Baumker Charitable Foundation, Inc.
2828 Barrington Drive
Toledo, OH 43606
(419) 535-6969

Operating grants; historical society; Pikeville College

Grants awarded to organizations located in Ohio, with an emphasis in Toledo.

Typical grant range: $500 to $7,000

476
Bicknell Fund
c/o Advisory Services, Inc.
1422 Euclid Avenue, Suite 1010
Cleveland, OH 44115
(216) 363-6482

Operating grants; Salvation Army; Visiting Nurse Association; Women's Community Fund; Youth Opportunities Unlimited; Laurel School; Planned Parenthood; Alcoholism Services of Cleveland; Animal Protection League; Boy Scouts; Goodwill Industries; Nature Conservancy

Typical grant range: $1,500 to $7,000

477
William Bingham Foundation
1250 Leader Building
Cleveland, OH 44114
(216) 781-3275

Operating grants; Trinity Repertory Company; Amos House (homeless); Environmental and Energy Study Institute

Typical grant range: $5,000 to $40,000

OHIO

478
Borden Foundation, Inc.
180 E. Broad Street, 34th Floor
Columbus, OH 43215
(614) 225-4340

Operating grants; disabled; cultural organizations; youth organizations; elderly; health organizations

Grants awarded to organizations located in areas of company operations.

Typical grant range: $3,000 to $20,000

479
Centerior Energy Foundation
6200 Oaktree Blvd.
Independence, OH 44131
(216) 479-4907

Operating grants; cultural organizations; social welfare; health organizations

Most grants awarded to organizations located in the Cleveland vicinity.

480
Chope Foundation, Inc.
Last minute update: this foundation has been terminated.

481
Cleveland Foundation
1422 Euclid Avenue, Suite 1400
Cleveland, OH 44115
(216) 861-3810

Operating grants; child welfare; historical societies; performing arts; education; minorities; disabled; community development; homeless; AIDS; African American Museum; Children's Defense Fund

Grants awarded to organizations located in the Cleveland vicinity.

Typical grant range: $1,000 to $75,000

482
Columbus Foundation
1234 E. Broad Street
Columbus, OH 43205
(614) 251-4000

Operating grants; Botanical Garden

Grants awarded to organizations located in the Columbus vicinity.

483
Dana Corporation Foundation
P.O. Box 1000
Toledo, OH 43697
(419) 535-4601

Operating grants; social welfare; health organizations; youth organizations; cultural organizations; community development

Grants awarded to organizations located in areas of company operations.

Typical grant range: $1,000 to $8,500

484
Charles H. Dater Foundation, Inc.
508 Atlas Bank Building
Cincinnati, OH 45202
(513) 241-1234

Operating grants; social welfare; youth organizations; Daycare Camp; Radio Reading Service

Grants awarded to organizations located in the Cincinnati vicinity.

Typical grant range: $1,000 to $11,000

485
Dayton Power & Light Company Foundation
Courthouse Plaza, S.W.
P.O. Box 1247
Dayton, OH 45402
(513) 259-7131

Operating grants; cultural organizations; social welfare; community development; health organizations

Typical grant range: $500 to $15,000

486
Eaton Charitable Fund
Eaton Corporation
Eaton Center
Cleveland, OH 44114
(216) 523-4822

Operating grants; social welfare; health organizations; cultural organizations

Grants awarded to organizations located in areas of company operations.

Typical grant range: $1,000 to $8,000

487
1525 Foundation
1525 National City Bank Building
Cleveland, OH 44114
(216) 696-4200

Operating grants; social welfare; environment; youth organizations; cultural organizations

Most grants awarded to organizations located in Cuyahoga County.

Typical grant range: $10,000 to $100,000

488
George Gund Foundation
1845 Guildhall Building
45 Prospect Avenue West
Cleveland, OH 44115
(216) 241-3114

Operating grants; cultural organizations; community development; environment; child welfare; minorities; homeless; women; youth organizations; AIDS

489
Hoover Foundation
101 E. Maple Street
North Canton, OH 44720
(216) 499-9200

Operating grants; hospitals; health organizations; social welfare; child welfare; environment; community development; higher education; cultural organizations; recreation; Educational Television; Out of Poverty Program; Homeless Center; Neighborhood Action Program; Council on Alcoholism; Junior Achievement/Junior League; American Lung Association; Center for the Arts; Habitat for Humanity

Most grants awarded to organizations located in Stark County.

Typical grant range: $10,000 to $80,000

490
George M. and Pamela S. Humphrey Fund
Advisory Services, Inc.
1010 Hanna Building, 1422 Euclid Ave.
Cleveland, OH 44115
(216) 363-6483

Operating grants; cultural organizations; community development; hospitals

Grants awarded to organizations located in Ohio.

Typical grant range: $2,000 to $12,000

491
Iddings Foundation
Kettering Tower, Suite 1620
Dayton, OH 45423
(513) 224-1773

Operating grants; disabled; environment; cultural organizations; health organizations

Most grants awarded to organizations located in Dayton.

Typical grant range: $2,000 to $15,000

OHIO

492
Kettering Family Foundation
1440 Kettering Tower
Dayton, OH 45423

Operating grants; cultural organizations; Trees for the Future; Council on Foundations

Typical grant range: $5,000 to $30,000

493
LTV Foundation Charitable and Educational Trust
c/o Society National Bank
P.O. Box 5937
Cleveland, OH 44101

Operating grants; cultural organizations; youth organizations; health organizations; community development

Grants awarded to organizations located in areas of company operations.

Typical grant range: $500 to $6,000

494
Lubrizol Foundation
29400 Lakeland Blvd.
Wickliffe, OH 44092
(216) 943-4200

Operating grants; youth organizations; cultural organizations; social welfare; disabled; health organizations

Grants awarded to organizations located in areas of company operations.

Typical grant range: $1,000 to $11,000

495
Elizabeth Ring Mather and William Gwinn Mather Fund
650 Citizens Building
850 Euclid Avenue
Cleveland, OH 44114
(216) 861-5341

Operating grants; Child Guidance Center; Children's Aid Society; Museum of Natural History; Scholarship Fund; Art Museum; Botanical Gardens; School of Music; Episcopal School; Nursing Services; County Day School; WCPN-Public Radio; Historical Society; Memorial Sloan Kettering Hospital; Musical Arts Association; Nature Conservancy; Planned Parenthood; United Way

496
S. Livingston Mather Charitable Trust
803 Tower East
20600 Chagrin Blvd.
Shaker Heights, OH 44122
(216) 942-6484

Operating grants; social welfare; environment; cultural organizations; disabled; child welfare

Typical grant range: $500 to $9,000

497
Charles Moerlein Foundation
c/o Fifth Third Bank
Dept. 00864
Cincinnati, OH 45263
(513) 579-6034

Operating grants; Center for Local Government

Grants awarded to organizations located in the Cincinnati vicinity.

Typical grant range: $7,000 to $15,000

OHIO

498
John P. Murphy Foundation
Tower City Center
Suite 610 Terminal Tower
50 Public Square
Cleveland, OH 44113
(216) 623-4770

Operating grants; cultural organizations; social welfare; youth organizations; health organizations

Grants awarded to organizations located in the Cleveland vicinity.

Typical grant range: $2,000 to $50,000

499
Nationwide Insurance Foundation
One Nationwide Plaza
Columbus, OH 43216
(614) 249-5095

Operating grants; cultural organizations; disabled; social welfare

Grants awarded to organizations located in areas of company operations, with an emphasis in Columbus.

Typical grant range: $5,000 to $65,000

500
Elisabeth Severance Prentiss Foundation
c/o National City Bank
P.O. Box 5756
Cleveland, OH 44101
(216) 575-2760

Operating grants; health organizations; hospitals; social welfare; disabled

Grants awarded to organizations located in the Cleveland vicinity.

501
Reeves Foundation
232-4 W. Third Street
P.O. Box 441
Dover, OH 44622
(216) 364-4660

Operating grants; Historical Society

Grants awarded to organizations located in Ohio, with an emphasis in Dover.

502
Reinberger Foundation
27600 Chagrin Blvd.
Cleveland, OH 44122
(216) 292-2790

Operating grants; symphony; cultural organizations; social welfare

Most grants awarded to organizations located in the Cleveland vicinity.

Typical grant range: $10,000 to $80,000

503
Richland County Foundation of Mansfield, Ohio
24 W. Third Street, Suite 100
Mansfield, OH 44902
(419) 525-3020

Operating grants; hospitals; health organizations; social welfare; youth organizations

Grants awarded to organizations located in Richland County.

504
Sears-Swetland Foundation
907 Park Building
Cleveland, OH 44114
(216) 241-6434

Operating grants; Alcoholism Services of Cleveland; Boy Scouts; Girl Scouts; Cleveland Museum of Art; Free Medical Clinic; Planned Parenthood; Salvation Army

Grants awarded to organizations located in the Cleveland vicinity.

Typical grant range: $500 to $3,000

505
Sherwin-Williams Foundation
101 Prospect Ave., NW, 12th Floor
Cleveland, OH 44115
(216) 566-2511

Operating grants; social welfare; health organizations; cultural organizations

Most grants awarded to organizations located in Cleveland.

506
Kelvin and Eleanor Smith Foundation
1100 National City Bank Bldg.
Cleveland, OH 44114
(216) 566-5500

Operating grants; performing arts; cultural organizations

Grants awarded to organizations located in the Cleveland vicinity.

Typical grant range: $5,000 to $40,000

507
Stocker Foundation
209 Sixth Street, Suite 25
Lorain, OH 44052
(216) 246-5719

Operating grants; social welfare; youth organizations; cultural organizations

Typical grant range: $2,000 to $12,000

508
Frank M. Tait Foundation
Courthouse Plaza, S.W., 10th Floor
Dayton, OH 45402
(513) 222-2401

Operating grants; cultural organizations; youth organizations; Alliance for Education

Grants awarded to organizations located in Montgomery County.

Typical grant range: $1,000 to $15,000

509
TRW Foundation
1900 Richmond Road
Cleveland, OH 44124
(216) 291-7166

Operating grants; disabled; social welfare; youth organizations; cultural organizations; hospitals; health organizations; minorities

Grants awarded to organizations located in areas of company operations, with an emphasis in Cleveland.

Typical grant range: $5,000 to $35,000

510
White Consolidated Industries Foundation, Inc.
c/o White Consolidated Industries, Inc.
11770 Berea Road
Cleveland, OH 44111
(216) 252-3700

Operating grants; cultural organizations; social welfare

Most grants awarded to organizations located in Cleveland and Columbus.

Typical grant range: $2,000 to $75,000

511
Thomas H. White Foundation
627 Hanna Building
1422 Euclid Avenue
Cleveland, OH 44115
(216) 696-7273

Operating grants; homeless; Food Bank; Hard Hatted Women

Grants awarded to organizations located in Cleveland.

Typical grant range: $1,000 to $35,000

512
Wolfe Associates Inc.
34 S. Third Street
Columbus, OH 43215
(614) 461-5220

Operating grants; health organizations; hospitals; social welfare; youth organizations; cultural organizations

Typical grant range: $2,000 to $20,000

OKLAHOMA

513
Mary K. Ashbrook Foundation for El Reno, Oklahoma
P.O. Box 627
El Reno, OK 73036

Operating grants; hospitals; health organizations; elderly; community development; Chamber of Commerce; Mobile Wheels of Reno

Grants awarded to organizations located in El Reno.

Typical grant range: $1,000 to $15,000

514
Charles B. Goddard Foundation
1000 Energy Center, Suite 102
P.O. Box 1485
Ardmore, OK 73402
(405) 226-6040

Operating grants; child welfare; community development; education; hospitals; health organizations

Typical grant range: $1,000 to $15,000

515
Harris Foundation, Inc.
6403 N.W. Grand Blvd., Suite 211
Oklahoma City, OK 73116
(405) 848-3371

Operating grants; social welfare; cultural organizations; animal welfare; youth organizations; health organizations; community development; disabled; Boy Scouts; Allied Arts Foundation; Crime Stoppers; Fellowship of Christian Athletes

Grants awarded to organizations located in Oklahoma.

Typical grant range: $1,000 to $20,000

516
Helmerich Foundation
1579 E. 21st Street
Tulsa, OK 74114
(918) 742-5531

Operating grants; cultural organizations; Tulsa Ballet Theatre; Retina Research Foundation

Grants awarded to organizations located in the Tulsa vicinity.

Typical grant range: $30,000 to $100,000

517
Kirkpatrick Foundation, Inc.
1300 N. Broadway Drive
Oklahoma City, OK 73103
(405) 235-5621

Operating grants; cultural organizations; social welfare

Grants awarded to organizations located in Oklahoma City.

518
Phillips Petroleum Foundation, Inc.
Phillips Building
Bartlesville, OK 74001
(918) 661-6248

Operating grants; youth organizations; social welfare; cultural organizations

Grants awarded to organizations located in areas of company operations.

Typical grant range: $1,000 to $20,000

519
C.W. Titus Foundation
1801 Philtower Building
Tulsa, OK 74103
(918) 582-8095

Operating grants; cultural organizations; social welfare; disabled; hospitals; health organizations

Typical grant range: $1,000 to $15,000

520
Anne and Henry Zarrow Foundation
Mid-Continent Tower
P.O. Box 1530
Tulsa, OK 74101
(918) 587-3391

Operating grants; disabled; social welfare; cultural organizations; health organizations

Grants awarded to organizations located in the Tulsa vicinity.

Typical grant range: $3,000 to $20,000

OREGON

521
Carpenter Foundation
711 E. Main Street, Suite 10
P.O. Box 816
Medford, OR 97501
(503) 772-5851

Operating grants; Grants Pass Family YMCA

Grants awarded to organizations located in Jackson and Josephine Counties.

Typical grant range: $2,000 to $15,000

522
Samuel S. Johnson Foundation
P.O. Box 356
Redmond, OR 97756
(503) 548-8104

Operating grants; cultural organizations; health organizations; social welfare; women; environment

Typical grant range: $400 to $1,500

523
Meyer Memorial Trust
1515 S.W. Fifth Ave., Suite 500
Portland, OR 97201
(503) 228-5512

Operating grants; cultural organizations; women; elderly; disabled; health organizations

Most grants awarded to organizations located in Oregon.

524
Oregon Community Foundation
621 S.W. Morrison, Suite 725
Portland, OR 97205
(503) 227-6846

Operating grants; social welfare; youth organizations; community development; disabled; cultural organizations; health organizations

Grants awarded to organizations located in Oregon.

Typical grant range: $1,000 to $20,000

525
Tektronix Foundation
P.O. Box 1000
Wilsonville, OR 97077
(503) 627-7084

Operating grants; social welfare; community development; health organizations

Grants awarded to organizations located in Oregon.

Typical grant range: $12,000 to $25,000

526
Rose E. Tucker Charitable Trust
900 S.W. Fifth Avenue
Portland, OR 97204
(503) 224-3380

Operating grants; social welfare; disabled; community development; performing arts; museums; health organizations; women; Tucker Maxon Oral School

Most grants awarded to organizations located in the Portland vicinity.

Typical grant range: $2,000 to $11,000

PENNSYLVANIA

527
Air Products Foundation
7201 Hamilton Blvd.
Allentown, PA 18195
(215) 481-8079

Operating grants; youth organizations; community development; social welfare; minorities

Grants awarded to organizations located in areas of company operations.

Typical grant range: $500 to $9,000

528
Alcoa Foundation
2202 Alcoa Building
425 Sixth Avenue
Pittsburgh, PA 15219
(412) 553-2343

Operating grants; cultural organizations; community development; youth organizations; social welfare

Grants awarded to organizations located in areas of company operations.

Typical grant range: $1,000 to $15,000

529
Arcadia Foundation
105 E. Logan Street
Norristown, PA 19401
(215) 275-8460

Operating grants; child welfare; elderly; disabled; health organizations; hospitals; environment

Grants awarded to organizations located in Pennsylvania.

Typical grant range: $1,000 to $25,000

530
Claude Worthington Benedum Foundation
1400 Benedum-Trees Building
Pittsburgh, PA 15222
(412) 288-0360

Operating grants; social welfare; health organizations; education; environment; cultural organizations

Typical grant range: $25,000 to $50,000

531
H.M. Bitner Charitable Trust
c/o Mellon Bank, N.A.
One Mellon Bank Center, Room 3845
Pittsburgh, PA 15258
(412) 234-4695

Operating grants; social welfare; cultural organizations; hospitals

Typical grant range: $500 to $4,000

532
CIGNA Foundation
One Liberty Place
1650 Market Street
Philadelphia, PA 19192
(215) 761-6055

Operating grants; performing arts; museums; health organizations

Typical grant range: $3,000 to $50,000

PENNSYLVANIA

533
Consolidated Natural Gas Company Foundation
c/o CNG Tower
625 Liberty Avenue
Pittsburgh, PA 15222
(412) 227-1200

Operating grants; youth organizations; health organizations; higher education; community development; social welfare; cultural organizations

Grants awarded to organizations located in areas of company operations.

Typical grant range: $1,000 to $30,000

534
William B. Dietrich Foundation
1811 Chestnut Street, Suite 304
Philadelphia, PA 19103
(215) 988-0050

Operating grants; environment; community development; cultural organizations; AIDS

Grants awarded to organizations located in Pennsylvania.

Typical grant range: $5,000 to $35,000

535
Dolfinger-McMahon Foundation
c/o Duane, Morris & Heckscher
One Liberty Place
Philadelphia, PA 19103
(215) 979-1768

Operating grants; health organizations; hospitals; social welfare; AIDS

Grants awarded to organizations located in Philadelphia.

Typical grant range: $2,000 to $12,000

536
Eden Foundation
4915 Monument Road
Philadelphia, PA 19131

Operating grants; historic preservation; Military Academy

Grants awarded to organizations located in the Philadelphia vicinity.

Typical grant range: $500 to $7,000

537
Grable Foundation
650 Smithfield Street, Suite 240
Pittsburgh, PA 15222
(412) 471-4550

Operating grants; social welfare; women; youth organizations

Typical grant range: $2,000 to $15,000

538
Grundy Foundation
680 Radcliffe Street
P.O. Box 701
Bristol, PA 19007
(215) 788-5460

Operating grants; social welfare; hospitals; community development; youth organizations

Grants awarded to organizations located in Bucks County.

539
Vira I. Heinz Endowment
30 CNG Tower
625 Liberty Avenue
Pittsburgh, PA 15222
(412) 391-5122

Operating grants; cultural organizations; education

Most grants awarded to organizations located in the Pittsburgh vicinity.

Typical grant range: $15,000 to $200,000

540
Henry L. Hillman Foundation
2000 Grant Building
Pittsburgh, PA 15219
(412) 338-3466

Operating grants; environment; youth organizations; cultural organizations; social welfare; health organizations

Most grants awarded to organizations located in the Pittsburgh vicinity.

Typical grant range: $2,000 to $20,000

541
T. James Kavanagh Foundation
57 Northwood Road
Newton Square, PA 19073
(215) 356-0743

Operating grants; health organizations; social welfare; Catholic organizations

Most grants awarded to organizations located in Pennsylvania.

Typical grant range: $500 to $3,000

542
Laurel Foundation
6th Floor North
Three Gateway Center
Pittsburgh, PA 15222
(412) 765-2400

Operating grants; social welfare; health organizations; cultural organizations

543
Mellon Bank Foundation
c/o Mellon Bank Corp.
One Mellon Bank Center, Suite 1830
Pittsburgh, PA 15258
(412) 234-2732

Operating grants; social welfare; community development; cultural organizations; health organizations

Grants awarded to organizations located in Southwestern Pennsylvania.

544
R.K. Mellon Family Foundation
P.O. Box 2930
Pittsburgh, PA 15230
(412) 392-2800

Operating grants; social welfare; health organizations; higher education; cultural organizations

Typical grant range: $5,000 to $35,000

545
Richard King Mellon Foundation
P.O. Box 2930
Pittsburgh, PA 15230
(412) 392-2800

Operating grants; social welfare; environment; community development; youth organizations

Most grants awarded to organizations located in Pittsburgh.

Typical grant range: $40,000 to $250,000

546
Grace S. and W. Linton Nelson Foundation
West Valley Business Center
940 W. Valley Road, Suite 1601
Wayne, PA 19087
(215) 975-9169

Operating grants; child welfare; youth organizations

Typical grant range: $5,000 to $35,000

547
Pew Charitable Trusts
One Commerce Square
2005 Market Street, Suite 1700
Philadelphia, PA 19103
(215) 575-9050

Operating grants; environment; performing arts; cultural organizations; community development; youth organizations; disabled; social welfare

PENNSYLVANIA

548
Philadelphia Foundation
1234 Market Street, Suite 1900
Philadelphia, PA 19107
(215) 563-6417

Operating grants; social welfare; disabled; cultural organizations; hospitals; health organizations; youth organizations

Most grants awarded to organizations located in the Philadelphia vicinity.

Typical grant range: $5,000 to $30,000

549
Harry Plankenhorn Foundation, Inc.
c/o Abram M. Snyder
R.D. 2
Cogan Station, PA 17728

Operating grants; youth organizations; social welfare; disabled; health organizations

Grants awarded to organizations located in Lycoming County.

Typical grant range: $1,000 to $20,000

550
PNC Bank Foundation
c/o PNC Bank, N.A.
Fifth Ave. and Wood St., 29th Fl.
Pittsburgh, PA 15222
(412) 762-3137

Operating grants; cultural organizations; social welfare; youth organizations; health organizations; community development

Typical grant range: $1,000 to $20,000

551
PPG Industries Foundation
One PPG Place
Pittsburgh, PA 15272
(412) 434-2962

Operating grants; cultural organizations; social welfare; youth organizations; health organizations

Grants awarded to organizations located in areas of company operations, with an emphasis in Pittsburgh.

552
Rockwell Foundation
c/o Pittsburgh Bank, C & I Trust Dept.
One Oliver Plaza, 27th Fl.
Pittsburgh, PA 15265
(412) 762-3390

Operating grants; environment; health organizations; social welfare; disabled; cultural organizations

Grants awarded to organizations located in Pennsylvania.

553
Scaife Family Foundation
Three Mellon Bank Center
525 William Penn Place, Suite 3900
Pittsburgh, PA 15219
(412) 392-2900

Operating grants; social welfare; health organizations; disabled

Typical grant range: $20,000 to $85,000

554
Sarah Scaife Foundation, Inc.
Three Mellon Bank Center
525 William Penn Place, Suite 3900
Pittsburgh, PA 15219
(412) 392-2900

Operating grants; Public Policy Center; Heritage Foundation

555
Shore Fund
c/o Mellon Bank, N.A.
P.O. Box 185
Pittsburgh, PA 15230
(412) 234-4695

Operating grants; hospitals; child welfare; higher education; environment

Grants awarded to organizations located in Pennsylvania.

Typical grant range: $1,000 to $30,000

PENNSYLVANIA

556
Ethel Sergeant Clark Smith Memorial Fund
101 Bryn Mawr Avenue, Suite 200
Bryn Mawr, PA 19010
(215) 525-9667

Operating grants; disabled; women; social welfare; cultural organizations; community development; health organizations; elderly

Grants awarded to organizations located in Delaware County.

Typical grant range: $5,000 to $40,000

557
Hoxie Harrison Smith Foundation
210 Fairlamb Avenue
Havertown, PA 19083
(215) 446-4651

Operating grants; elderly; child welfare; disabled; hospitals

558
W.W. Smith Charitable Trust
101 Bryn Mawr Avenue, Suite 200
Bryn Mawr, PA 19010
(215) 525-9667

Operating grants; elderly; minorities; child welfare; women; disabled; social welfare; homeless; AIDS

Typical grant range: $10,000 to $35,000

559
SPS Foundation
c/o SPS Technologies
301 Highland Avenue
Jenkintown, PA 19046

Operating grants; cultural organizations; youth organizations; community development; health organizations

Typical grant range: $200 to $2,500

560
Louis L. Stott Foundation
c/o Morgan, Lewis & Bockius
2000 One Logan Square
Philadelphia, PA 19103
(215) 963-5281

Operating grants; environment; health organizations; social welfare

Typical grant range: $1,000 to $6,500

561
Harry C. Trexler Trust
33 S. Seventh Street, Suite 205
Allentown, PA 18101
(215) 434-9645

Operating grants; youth organizations; social welfare; disabled; cultural organizations; health organizations

Grants awarded to organizations located in Lehigh County.

Typical grant range: $12,000 to $30,000

562
USX Foundation, Inc.
600 Grant Street
Pittsburgh, PA 15219
(412) 433-5237

Operating grants; cultural organizations; youth organizations; health organizations; social welfare; elderly; disabled; United Way

Grants awarded to organizations located in areas of company operations.

Typical grant range: $3,000 to $40,000

563
Henrietta Tower Wurts Memorial
Fidelity Bank, N.A.
135 S. Broad Street
Philadelphia, PA 19109
(215) 985-8361

Operating grants; child welfare; women; community development; social welfare; health organizations; youth organizations

Grants awarded to organizations located in Philadelphia.

564
Wyomissing Foundation, Inc.
1015 Penn Avenue
Wyomissing, PA 19610
(215) 376-7496

Operating grants; social welfare; environment; youth organizations; women; cultural organizations; health organizations; social welfare

Grants awarded to organizations located in Berks County.

Typical grant range: $2,000 to $22,000

PUERTO RICO

565
Puerto Rico Community Foundation
Royal Bank Center Building, Suite 1417
Hato Rey, PR 00917
(809) 751-3822

Operating grants; cultural organizations; health organizations; elderly; AIDS

Grants awarded to organizations located in Puerto Rico.

Typical grant range: $5,000 to $35,000

RHODE ISLAND

566
Cranston Foundation
1381 Cranston Street
Cranston, RI 02920
(401) 943-4800

Operating grants; hospitals; health organizations; cultural organizations; disabled; social welfare

567
Providence Journal Charitable Foundation
75 Fountain Street
Providence, RI 02902
(401) 277-7286

Operating grants; cultural organizations; youth organizations

Grants awarded to organizations located in Rhode Island.

Typical grant range: $1,500 to $20,000

568
Rhode Island Foundation/Rhode Island Community Foundation
70 Elm Street
Providence, RI 02903
(401) 274-4564

Operating grants; social welfare; disabled; elderly; health organizations; AIDS

Grants awarded to organizations located in Rhode Island.

SOUTH CAROLINA

569
Saul Alexander Foundation
c/o South Carolina National Bank, Trust Dept.
P.O. Box 71505
Charleston Heights, SC 29415
(803) 744-8261

Operating grants; Museum of Summerville; Public Library; Meals on Wheels; Summerville Preservation Society; Christian Jewish Council; Star Gospel Mission; Hospice of Charleston; Crisis Ministry; Jenkins Orphanage; Jewish Social Services; Charleston Symphony Orchestra; Ebony City Soccer Club; Gibbs-Carolina Arts Association; Salvation Army; Youth Services

570
Fullerton Foundation
515 W. Buford Street
Gaffney, SC 29340
(803) 489-6678

Operating grants; Salvation Army

Typical grant range: $10,000 to $85,000

571
Hamrick Mills Foundation, Inc.
P.O. Box 48
Gaffney, SC 29342

Operating grants; Cherokee County Public Library; Fellowship of Christian Athletes; National Bible Association; Meals on Wheels; Boys and Girls Clubs; Special Olympics; United Way; Cherokee Suicide Intervention Center; Cherokee Children's Home; South Carolina Council on Economic Education; American Cancer Society

Grants awarded to organizations located in Cherokee County.

Typical grant range: $500 to $6,000

572
Joanna Foundation
P.O. Box 21537
Charleston, SC 29413

Operating grants; cultural organizations; social welfare; disabled; environment

Grants awarded to organizations located in South Carolina.

573
Spartanburg County Foundation
320 E. Main Street
Spartanburg, SC 29302
(803) 582-0138

Operating grants; Hatcher Botanical Gardens

Grants awarded to organizations located in Spartanburg county.

Typical grant range: $1,000 to $12,000

574
Springs Foundation
P.O. Drawer 460
Lancaster, SC 29721
(803) 286-2196

Operating grants; hospitals; recreation

Typical grant range: $3,000 to $30,000

575
Trident Community Foundation
456 King Street
Charleston, SC 29403
(803) 723-3635

Operating grants; social welfare; Low Country Releaf (they plant trees); Charleston Affordable Housing

Typical grant range: $500 to $7,000

SOUTH DAKOTA

576
South Dakota Community Foundation
207 East Capitol
P.O. Box 296
Pierre, SD 57501
(605) 224-1025

Operating grants; museums; Heritage Center; Turn About, Inc. (parent/child center)

Grants awarded to organizations located in South Dakota.

Typical grant range: $500 to $10,000

TENNESSEE

577
HCA Foundation
c/o Hospital Corp. of America
One Park Plaza, P.O. Box 550
Nashville, TN 37202-0550
(615) 320-2165

Operating grants; social welfare; cultural organizations; Nashville Area Community Foundation; United Way

Grants awarded to organizations located in areas of company operations, with an emphasis in Nashville.

Typical grant range: $1,000 to $25,000

578
William P. and Marie R. Lowenstein Foundation
100 N. Main Building, Suite 3020
Memphis, TN 38103
(901) 525-5744

Operating grants; health organizations; youth organizations; social welfare; disabled; Jewish organizations

Most grants awarded to organizations located in Tennessee.

Typical grant range: $250 to $5,000

579
Lyndhurst Foundation
Tallan Building, Suite 701
100 W. Martin Luther King Blvd.
Chattanooga, TN 37402
(615) 756-0767

Operating grants; community development; cultural organizations; environment; youth organizations

Most grants awarded to organizations located in Chattanooga.

Typical grant range: $20,000 to $100,000

580
Maclellan Foundation, Inc.
Provident Building, Suite 501
Chattanooga, TN 37402
(615) 755-1366

Operating grants; Churches; International Urban Association; Christian College; Bible Study School; Ministries; Youth for Christ; Allied Arts; Clinical Pastoral Care; Family Action Coalition; Rescue Mission; Theological Seminary; Bible Institute; Christian School; Children's Advocacy Center; Fellowship of Christian Athletes

Grants awarded to organizations located in the Chattanooga vicinity.

Most grants awarded to Protestant related organizations.

Typical grant range: $30,000 to $100,000

581
R.J. Maclellan Charitable Trust
Provident Building, Suite 501
Chattanooga, TN 37402
(615) 755-1366

Operating grants; social welfare; child welfare; education; cultural organizations

Most grants awarded to organizations located in Chattanooga.

Most grants awarded to Protestant related organizations.

Typical grant range: $15,000 to $125,000

582
Plough Foundation
6077 Primacy Parkway, Suite 230
Memphis, TN 38119
(901) 761-9180

Operating grants; social welfare; cultural organizations

Grants awarded to organizations located in the Memphis vicinity.

Typical grant range: $15,000 to $100,000

583
Justin and Valere Potter Foundation
c/o NationsBank Personal Trust
One NationsBank Plaza M-7
Nashville, TN 37239
(615) 749-3586

Operating grants; cultural organizations; social welfare

Grants awarded to organizations located in Nashville.

Typical grant range: $15,000 to $85,000

584
Tonya Memorial Foundation
American National Bank and Trust Company
736 Market Street
Chattanooga, TN 37402

Operating grants; Center City Corporation; McCallie School

Grants awarded to organizations located in Chattanooga.

Few operating grants available.

Typical grant range: $5,000 to $200,000

585
Woods-Greer Foundation
American National Bank and Trust Co.
736 Market Street, P.O. Box 1638
Chattanooga, TN 37401
(615) 757-3203

Operating budgets; Community Action Center; Churches; Center for Public Policy; Neighborhood House; Theological Seminary; Music Center; Episcopal Radio and T.V. Foundation; Botanical Gardens and Fine Arts Center

Typical grant range: $1,000 to $8,000

TEXAS

586
Abell-Hanger Foundation
P.O. Box 430
Midland, TX 79702
(915) 684-6655

Operating grants; disabled; cultural organizations; social welfare; elderly; youth organizations; hospice; health organizations

Grants awarded to organizations located in Texas.

Typical grant range: $15,000 to $75,000

587
Abercrombie Foundation
5005 Riverway, Suite 500
Houston, TX 77056
(713) 627-2500

Operating grants; social welfare; cultural organizations; all levels of education; health organizations

Grants awarded to organizations located in Houston.

588
Amini Foundation
8000 IH-Ten West, Suite 820
San Antonio, TX 78230

Operating grants; child welfare; youth organizations; cultural organizations

Most grants awarded to organizations located in San Antonio.

TEXAS

589
Brown Foundation, Inc.
2117 Welch Avenue
P.O. Box 130646
Houston, TX 77219
(713) 523-6867

Operating grants; performing arts; museums; health organizations; child welfare

Most grants awarded to organizations located in the Houston vicinity.

Typical grant range: $15,000 to $120,000

590
H.L. & Elizabeth M. Brown Foundation
6300 Ridglea Place, Suite 1118
Ft. Worth, TX 76116

Operating grants; health organizations; hospitals

Grants awarded to organizations located in Texas.

Typical grant range: $500 to $5,000

591
Burkitt Foundation
5847 San Felipe, Suite 4290
Houston, TX 77057
(713) 780-7638

Operating grants; social welfare; health organizations; Catholic related organizations

Typical grant range: $1,000 to $7,000

592
Effie and Wofford Cain Foundation
4131 Spicewood Springs Road, Suite A-1
Austin, TX 78759
(512) 346-7490

Operating grants; social welfare; youth organizations; cultural organizations; disabled; Churches

Grants awarded to organizations located in Texas.

Typical grant range: $5,000 to $75,000

593
Gordon and Mary Cain Foundation
Eight Greenway Plaza, Suite 702
Houston, TX 77046
(713) 960-9283

Operating grants; child welfare; social welfare; performing arts; museums; health organizations

Grants awarded to organizations located in Houston.

594
Clayton Fund, Inc.
First City, Texas-Houston
P.O. Box 809
Houston, TX 77001

Operating grants; social welfare; cultural organizations

Grants awarded to organizations located in Texas.

Typical grant range: $3,000 to $30,000

595
Cockrell Foundation
1600 Smith, Suite 4600
Houston, TX 77002
(713) 651-1271

Operating grants; health organizations; women; animal welfare; child welfare

Grants awarded to organizations located in the Houston vicinity.

Typical grant range: $5,000 to $50,000

596
Community Foundation of Abilene
500 Chestnut, Suite 1509
P.O. Box 1001
Abilene, TX 79604
(915) 676-3883

Operating grants; social welfare; health organizations; youth organizations; Medical Care Mission

Grants awarded to organizations located in the Abilene vicinity.

Typical grant range: $1,000 to $12,000

597
Denton A. Cooley Foundation
6624 Fannin, Suite 2700
Houston, TX 77030
(713) 799-2700

Operating grants; health organizations; hospitals

Grants awarded to organizations located in the Houston vicinity.

Typical grant range: $250 to $7,000

598
Raymond Dickson Foundation
P.O. Box 406
Hallettsville, TX 77964
(512) 798-2531

Operating grants; child welfare; hospitals; health organizations

Grants awarded to organizations located in Texas.

Typical grant range: $1,000 to $7,000

599
Dorset Foundation, Inc.
412 Bank One Bldg.
Sherman, TX 75090

Operating grants; hospices; child welfare

Grants awarded to organizations located in Grayson County.

Few grants awarded.

Typical grant range: $2,000 to $20,000

600
James R. Dougherty, Jr. Foundation
P.O. Box 640
Beeville, TX 78104
(512) 358-3560

Operating grants; social welfare; health organizations; community development; animal welfare; drug abuse; disabled; Muscular Dystrophy Association

Grants awarded to organizations located in Texas.

Typical grant range: $1,000 to $4,000

601
J.E.S. Edwards Foundation
4413 Cumberland Road North
Fort Worth, TX 76116
(817) 737-6924

Operating grants; abused women; social welfare; youth organizations

Grants awarded to organizations located in Fort Worth.

Typical grant range: $1,000 to $9,000

602
Ellwood Foundation
P.O. Box 52482
Houston, TX 77052
(713) 652-0613

Operating grants; hospitals; health organizations; youth organizations; social welfare

Most grants awarded to organizations located in the Houston vicinity.

Typical grant range: $5,000 to $50,000

603
Enron Foundation
P.O. Box 1188
Houston, TX 77251
(713) 853-5400

Operating grants; cultural organizations; social welfare

Grants awarded to organizations located in areas of company operations.

Typical grant range: $2,000 to $25,000

604
Favrot Foundation
909 Wirt Road, Suite 101
Houston, TX 77024
(713) 956-4009

Operating grants; social welfare; youth organizations; animal welfare

Typical grant range: $5,000 to $40,000

TEXAS

605
Leland Fikes Foundation, Inc.
3050 Lincoln Plaza
500 N. Akard
Dallas, TX 75201
(214) 754-0144

Operating grants; hospitals; health organizations; social welfare; disabled; homeless; museums; performing arts

Grants awarded to organizations located in Dallas.

Typical grant range: $10,000 to $25,000

606
First Interstate Foundation of Texas
1000 Louisiana Street
P.O. Box 3326, MS No. 584
Houston, TX 77253
(713) 250-1850

Operating grants; Shriners Hospital for Crippled Children

607
Fleming Foundation
500 W. Seventh Street, Suite 1007
Ft. Worth, TX 76102

Operating grants; social welfare; youth organizations; Protestant related organizations

Most grants awarded to organizations located in the Ft. Worth vicinity.

Typical grant range: $1,000 to $25,000

608
George Foundation
207 S. Third Street
P.O. Drawer C
Richmond, TX 77469
(713) 342-6109

Operating grants; health organizations; social welfare; youth organizations; community development

Most grants awarded to organizations located in Ft. Bend County.

Typical grant range: $10,000 to $60,000

609
Paul and Mary Haas Foundation
P.O. Box 2928
Corpus Christi, TX 78403
(512) 887-6955

Operating grants; social welfare; disabled; youth organizations

Grants awarded to organizations located in the Corpus Christi vicinity.

Typical grant range: $2,000 to $11,000

610
Ewing Halsell Foundation
711 Navarro Street, Suite 537
San Antonio, TX 78205
(210) 223-2640

Operating grants; cultural organizations; museums; health organizations; social welfare

Most grants awarded to organizations located in San Antonio.

Typical grant range: $1,000 to $40,000

611
Houston Endowment, Inc.
600 Travis, Suite 6400
Houston, TX 77002
(713) 238-8100

Operating grants; social welfare; health organizations; youth organizations

Grants awarded to organizations located in Texas.

Typical grant range: $5,000 to $250,000

612
Ben E. Keith Foundation Trust
c/o Bank One
P.O. Box 2050
Ft. Worth, TX 76113
(817) 884-4161

Operating grants; social welfare; cultural organizations

Grants awarded to organizations located in Texas.

613
Harris and Eliza Kempner Fund
P.O. Box 119
Galveston, TX 77553
(409) 765-6671

Operating grants; disabled; social welfare; performing arts; museums; environment; health organizations; AIDS

Grants awarded to organizations located in Galveston.

Typical grant range: $1,500 to $8,500

614
Kimberly-Clark Foundation, Inc.
P.O. Box 619100
Dallas, TX 75261
(214) 830-1200

Operating grants; cultural organizations; social welfare

Grants awarded to organizations located in areas of company operations.

Typical grant range: $7,500 to $50,000

615
Marcia and Otto Koehler Foundation
c/o NationsBank
P.O. Box 688
San Antonio, TX 78293

Operating grants; social welfare; youth organizations; cultural organizations

Grants awarded to organizations located in the San Antonio vicinity.

Typical grant range: $4,000 to $20,000

616
Eugene McDermott Foundation
3808 Euclid
Dallas, TX 75205
(214) 521-2924

Operating grants; performing arts; zoo; community development; child welfare; disabled; United Methodist Church; Museum of African-American Life and Culture; United Way

Grants awarded to organizations located in Dallas.

Typical grant range: $2,500 to $25,000

617
Robert E. and Evelyn McKee Foundation
P.O. Box 220599
6006 N. Mesa Street, Suite 906
El Paso, TX 79913
(915) 581-4025

Operating grants; hospitals; youth organizations

Most grants awarded to organizations located in El Paso.

618
Meadows Foundation, Inc.
Wilson Historic Block
3003 Swiss Avenue
Dallas, TX 75204
(214) 826-9431

Operating grants; homeless; minorities; women; disabled; performing arts; health organizations; child welfare; environment

Grants awarded to organizations located in Texas.

Typical grant range: $25,000 to $80,000

TEXAS

619
Harry S. Moss Heart Trust
c/o NationsBank
P.O. Box 831041
Dallas, TX 75283
(214) 508-2041

Operating grants; heart disease including hospitals, health organizations, and Medical Schools

Most grants awarded to organizations located in Dallas.

Typical grant range: $25,000 to $175,000

620
Kathryn O'Connor Foundation
One O'Connor Plaza, Suite 1100
Victoria, TX 77901
(512) 578-6271

Operating grants; health organizations; higher education; hospitals; hospices; cultural organizations; Public Library; Churches

Typical grant range: $15,000 to $40,000

621
Alvin and Lucy Owsley Foundation
3000 One Shell Plaza
Houston, TX 77002
(713) 229-1271

Operating grants; social welfare; disabled; health organizations

Grants awarded to organizations located in Texas.

Typical grant range: $500 to $3,000

622
Sid W. Richardson Foundation
309 Main Street
Fort Worth, TX 76102
(817) 336-0494

Operating grants; cultural organizations; social welfare; Northside Inter-Church Agency; Botanical Research Institute

Grants awarded to organizations located in Texas.

Typical grant range: $10,000 to $125,000

623
Rockwell Fund, Inc.
1360 Post Oak Blvd., Suite 780
Houston, TX 77056
(713) 629-9022

Operating grants; cultural organizations; low-income families, homeless; Houston Area Women's Center; Mental Health Association; Planned Parenthood; Saint Michael Catholic Church; Association for Community Television

Grants awarded to organizations located in the Houston vicinity.

Typical grant range: $10,000 to $25,000

624
San Antonio Area Foundation
530 McCullough, Suite 600
San Antonio, TX 78215
(210) 225-2243

Operating grants; social welfare; health organizations; disabled; animal welfare

Grants awarded to organizations located in the San Antonio vicinity.

Typical grant range: $500 to $15,000

625
Harold Simmons Foundation
Three Lincoln Center
5430 LBJ Freeway, Suite 1700
Dallas, TX 75240

Operating grants; cultural organizations; social welfare; youth organizations; community development

Grants awarded to organizations located in the Dallas vicinity.

Typical grant range: $2,000 to $20,000

626
Swalm Foundation
8707 Katy Freeway, Suite 300
Houston, TX 77024
(713) 464-1321

Operating grants; health organizations; social welfare; Ministry

Grants awarded to organizations located in Texas.

Typical grant range: $1,000 to $25,000

627
Trull Foundation
404 Fourth Street
Palacios, TX 77465
(512) 972-5241

Operating grants; social welfare; disabled; minorities; health organizations; community development; Protestant related organizations; AIDS

628
Rachael & Ben Vaughan Foundation
P.O. Box 1579
Corpus Christi, TX 78403
(512) 241-2890

Operating grants; health organizations; women; environment; Austin Children's Museum; Planned Parenthood; Food Bank; Goodwill Industries; Center for Hearing Impaired Children; AIDS Services of Austin

Typical grant range: $500 to $7,000

629
Wortham Foundation
2727 Allen Parkway, Suite 2000
Houston, TX 77019
(713) 526-8849

Operating grants; performing arts; youth organizations; community development; United Way

Grants awarded to organizations located in the Houston vicinity.

UTAH

630
Ruth Eleanor Bamberger and John Ernest Bamberger Memorial Foundation
1201 Walker Building
Salt Lake City, UT 84111
(801) 364-2045

Operating grants; health organizations; hospitals; wildlife; youth organizations

Grants awarded to organizations located in Utah.

Typical grant range: $500 to $11,000

631
Castle Foundation
c/o West One Trust Co.
P.O. Box 3058
Salt Lake City, UT 84110
(801) 534-6085

Operating grants; higher education; social welfare; hospice; health organizations; child welfare; National Society for the Prevention of Blindness

Grants awarded to organizations located in Utah.

Typical grant range: $1,000 to $7,000

632
Marriner S. Eccles Foundation
701 Deseret Building
79 S. Main Street
Salt Lake City, UT 84111
(801) 322-0116

Operating grants; social welfare; youth organizations; cultural organizations; women; health organizations

Grants awarded to organizations located in Utah.

Typical grant range: $3,000 to $30,000

VERMONT

633
Canaan Foundation for Christian Education
R. R. One
P.O. Box 113
Woodstock, VT 05091
(802) 457-3990

Operating grants; Christian School; Pregnancy Center; Churches

634
Mortimer R. Proctor Trust
Green Mountain Bank, Trust Dept.
P.O. Box 669
Rutland, VT 05701
(802) 775-2525

Operating grants; cultural organizations; social welfare

Typical grant range: $2,000 to $20,000

VIRGINIA

635
Beazley Foundation, Inc.
3720 Brighton Street
Portsmouth, VA 23707
(804) 393-1605

Operating grants; Portsmouth Crime Line; Union Mission; Tidewater AIDS Crisis Task Force; Virginia Baptist Children's Home; Children's Hospital of the Kings Daughters; Family Shelter; Goodwill Industries; Diabetes Institutes Foundation; Mt. Hermon Athletic Association

636
Freedom Forum
1101 Wilson Blvd.
Arlington, VA 22209

Operating grants; higher education (journalism); minorities; women; social welfare

Typical grant range: $3,000 to $85,000

637
Memorial Foundation for Children
P.O. Box 8342
Richmond, VA 23226

Operating grants; child welfare; disabled; cultural organizations

Grants awarded to organizations located in the Richmond vicinity.

Grants awarded to organizations helping children.

Typical grant range: $5,000 to $22,000

638
Norfolk Southern Foundation
Three Commercial Place
Norfolk, VA 23510
(804) 629-2650

Operating grants; performing arts; museums; social welfare

Typical grant range: $1,000 to $35,000

639
Theresa A. Thomas Memorial Foundation
c/o Sovran Center
1111 E. Main Street, 21st Floor
Richmond, VA 23219

Operating grants; health organizations; Rescue Squad

Grants awarded to organizations located in Virginia.

Typical grant range: $5,000 to $75,000

640
J. Edwin Treakle Foundation, Inc.
P.O. Box 1157
Gloucester, VA 23061

Operating grants; Churches; Washington National Cathedral; American Red Cross

Grants awarded to organizations located in Virginia.

Typical grant range: $1,000 to $7,500

641
Universal Leaf Foundation
Hamilton Street at Broad
P.O. Box 25099
Richmond, VA 23260
(804) 359-9311

Operating grants; social welfare; health organizations; cultural organizations; animal welfare

Grants awarded to organizations located in Virginia.

Typical grant range: $500 to $5,000

642
Washington Forrest Foundation
2300 S. Ninth Street
Arlington, VA 22204
(703) 920-3688

Operating grants; social welfare; health organizations; cultural organizations

Grants awarded to organizations located in Northern Virginia.

Typical grant range: $1,000 to $7,000

WASHINGTON

643
Clifford Braden Foundation
P.O. Box 1757
Walla Walla, WA 99362
(509) 527-3500

Operating grants; higher education; museums; animal welfare; YMCA

644
Bullitt Foundation, Inc.
1212 Minor Ave.
Seattle, WA 98101
(206) 343-0807

Operating grants; environment

Typical grant range: $10,000 to $60,000

645
Ben B. Cheney Foundation, Inc.
1201 Pacific Ave., Suite 1600
Tacoma, WA 98402
(206) 572-2442

Operating grants; higher education

Typical grant range: $2,000 to $45,000

646
Forest Foundation
820 A Street, Suite 345
Tacoma, WA 98402
(206) 627-1634

Operating grants; Nature Conservancy; Center for Contemporary Art; Youth Symphony Association; Campaign for Puget Sound; Washington Council for Economic Education

Typical grant range: $2,000 to $30,000

647
Greater Tacoma Community Foundation
P.O. Box 1995
Tacoma, WA 98401
(206) 383-5622

Operating grants; social welfare; cultural organizations

Grants awarded to organizations located in Pierce County.

Typical grant range: $500 to $8,000

648
Matlock Foundation
1201 Third Avenue, Suite 4900
Seattle, WA 98101
(206) 224-5196

Operating grants; museums; performing arts; child welfare; health organizations; higher education; disabled; AIDS; Bay Area Women's Philharmonic; Food Bank; Junior Achievement; Planned Parenthood; Children's Orthopedic Hospital Foundation

649
Medina Foundation
1300 Norton Building
801 Second Avenue, 13th Floor
Seattle, WA 98104
(206) 464-5231

Operating grants; social welfare; disabled; cultural organizations; youth organizations

Grants awarded to organizations located in the Seattle vicinity.

Typical grant range: $5,000 to $20,000

650
New Horizon Foundation
820 A Street, Suite 345
Tacoma, WA 98402
(206) 627-1634

Operating grants; social welfare; cultural organizations

Typical grant range: $2,500 to $25,000

651
Norcliffe Foundation
First Interstate Center
999 Third Avenue, Suite 1006
Seattle, WA 98104

Operating grants; health organizations; social welfare; elderly; disabled

Grants awarded to organizations located in the Seattle vicinity.

Typical grant range: $500 to $20,000

652
Sequoia Foundation
820 A Street, Suite 345
Tacoma, WA 98402
(206) 627-1634

Operating grants; Junior Achievement; Boy Scouts; Art Museum; United Way; Foundation Center; World Wildlife; Food Research and Action; Conservation International Foundation

Typical grant range: $5,000 to $60,000

653
Skinner Foundation
1326 Fifth Avenue, Suite 711
Seattle, WA 98101
(206) 623-6480

Operating grants; social welfare; cultural organizations; health organizations; child welfare; disabled

Grants awarded to organizations located in areas of company operations (Skinner Corporation).

Typical grant range: $1,000 to $11,000

WEST VIRGINIA

654
Greater Kanawha Valley Foundation
1426 Kanawha Blvd., East
Charleston, WV 25301
(304) 346-3620

Operating grants; social welfare; disabled; performing arts; museums; health organizations; youth organizations

Grants awarded to organizations located in Greater Kanawha Valley.

Typical grant range: $1,000 to $14,000

655
Sarah and Pauline Maier Foundation, Inc.
P.O. Box 6190
Charleston, WV 25362
(304) 343-2201

Operating grants; higher education; cultural organizations

Grants awarded to organizations located in West Virginia.

Typical grant range: $10,000 to $65,000

WISCONSIN

656
Judd S. Alexander Foundation, Inc.
500 Third Street, Suite 509
P.O. Box 2137
Wausau, WI 54402
(715) 845-4556

Operating grants; cultural organizations; youth organizations; recreation; social welfare

Grants awarded to organizations located in Marathon County.

Typical grant range: $2,000 to $20,000

657
Badger Meter Foundation, Inc.
4545 W. Brown Deer Road
Milwaukee, WI 53223
(414) 355-0400

Operating grants; social welfare; cultural organizations

Grants awarded to organizations located in the Milwaukee vicinity.

658
Bucyrus-Erie Foundation, Inc.
1100 Milwaukee Avenue
S. Milwaukee, WI 53172
(414) 768-5005

Operating grants; youth organizations; social welfare; hospitals

Grants awarded to organizations located in the Milwaukee vicinity.

659
Patrick and Anna M. Cudahy Fund
P.O. Box 11978
Milwaukee, WI 53211
(708) 866-0760

Operating grants; cultural organizations; social welfare; disabled; youth organizations

Typical grant range: $3,000 to $25,000

660
CUNA Mutual Insurance Group Charitable Foundation, Inc.
5910 Mineral Point Road
Madison, WI 53705
(608) 231-7314

Operating grants; community development; health organizations; disabled; cultural organizations

Grants awarded to organizations located in Wisconsin.

661
Elizabeth Elser Doolittle Charitable Trust No. 1
c/o Foley & Lardner
777 E. Wisconsin Avenue
Milwaukee, WI 53202

Operating grants; health organizations; social welfare; disabled; cultural organizations; environment

Most grants awarded to organizations located in Wisconsin.

Typical grant range: $1,000 to $8,000

662
Carl and Elisabeth Eberbach Foundation, Inc.
c/o Firstar Trust Co.
P.O. Box 2054
Milwaukee, WI 53201

Operating grants; health organizations; hospitals; performing arts; museums

Most grants awarded to organizations located in the Milwaukee vicinity.

Typical grant range: $250 to $3,500

WISCONSIN

663
Ralph Evinrude Foundation, Inc.
c/o Quarles and Brady
411 E. Wisconsin Avenue
Milwaukee, WI 53202
(414) 277-5000

Operating grants; environment; youth organizations; cultural organizations; education; health organizations

Grants awarded to organizations located in Milwaukee.

Typical grant range: $500 to $4,000

664
Gardner Foundation
111 E. Wisconsin Avenue, Suite 1508
Milwaukee, WI 53202
(414) 272-0383

Operating grants; health organizations; social welfare; cultural organizations

Grants awarded to organizations located in the Milwaukee vicinity.

Typical grant range: $500 to $4,500

665
Madison Community Foundation
615 E. Washington Avenue
Madison, WI 53703
(608) 255-0503

Operating grants; social welfare; elderly; disabled; cultural organizations; health organizations; youth organizations

Grants awarded to organizations located in the Madison vicinity.

Typical grant range: $1,000 to $25,000

666
Faye McBeath Foundation
1020 North Broadway
Milwaukee, WI 53202
(414) 272-2626

Operating grants; disabled; social welfare; child welfare; health organizations; AIDS

Grants awarded to organizations located in Wisconsin, with an emphasis in Milwaukee.

Typical grant range: $10,000 to $40,000

667
Northwestern National Insurance Foundation
18650 W. Corporate Drive
Brookfield, WI 53005
(414) 792-3100

Operating grants; Museum of Natural History; Public Library; Public Radio; Public Television; Milwaukee Symphony Orchestra; Zoological Society; Historic Sites Foundation; Easter Seal Society; Jr. Achievement; United Way; American Cancer Society; Big Brothers/Big Sisters; Carol College; Children's Hospital

Grants awarded to organizations located in areas of company operations.

668
L.E. Phillips Family Foundation, Inc.
3925 N. Hastings Way
Eau Claire, WI 54703
(715) 839-2139

Operating grants; social welfare; cultural organizations; Jewish organizations; United Way

Typical grant range: $500 to $11,000

669
Siebert Lutheran Foundation, Inc.
2600 N. Mayfair Road, Suite 390
Wauwatosa, WI 53226
(414) 257-2656

Operating grants; social welfare; all levels of education; Churches

Grants awarded to organizations located in Wisconsin.

Grants awarded to Lutheran related organizations.

Typical grant range: $3,500 to $10,000

670
SNC Foundation, Inc.
101 Waukau Avenue
Oshkosh, WI 54901

Operating grants; higher education; women; Symphony Orchestra; Opera House; Confront Addiction Now; Boys Ranch; Senior Center; Medical Center; Community Health Care Foundation; Rowing Club One; City of Edensburg; Boys and Girls Club

Grants awarded to organizations located in Oshkosh.

Most grants awarded to preselected organizations.

Typical grant range: $100 to $2,500

671
Stackner Family Foundation, Inc.
411 E. Wisconsin Avenue
Milwaukee, WI 53202
(414) 277-5000

Operating grants; disabled; social welfare; health organizations; minorities; youth organizations

Grants awarded to organizations located in the Milwaukee vicinity.

Typical grant range: $1,500 to $12,000

672
Wisconsin Power and Light Foundation, Inc.
222 W. Washington Avenue
Madison, WI 53703
(608) 252-3181

Operating grants; performing arts; museums; health organizations; social welfare

Grants awarded to organizations located in areas of company operations.

Typical grant range: $150 to $2,500

673
Wisconsin Public Service Foundation, Inc.
700 N. Adams Street
Green Bay, WI 54301
(414) 433-1464

Operating grants; social welfare; health organizations; cultural organizations

Most grants awarded to organizations located in Wisconsin.

Typical grant range: $250 to $8,000

WYOMING

674
Tom and Helen Tonkin Foundation
c/o Norwest Bank Wyoming, Casper, N.A.
P.O. Box 2799
Casper, WY 82602
(307) 266-1100

Operating grants; grants awarded to organizations supporting youth (under 21) in the following areas: disabled, social welfare, health

Grants awarded to organizations located in Wyoming.

Typical grant range: $1,000 to $8,000

Appendix A
Bibliography of State and Local Foundation Directories
Compiled by Elizabeth McKenty

ALABAMA Birmingham Public Library. *Alabama Foundation Directory*. Birmingham, AL: Birmingham Public Library, 1990. Based primary on 990-PF returns filed with the IRS by 362 foundations. Available from the Birmingham Public Library, 2100 Park Place, Birmingham, AL 35203. Tel: (205) 266-3600.

ALASKA No directory.

ARIZONA Junior League of Phoenix. *Arizona Foundation Directory*. 3rd ed. Phoenix, AZ: Junior League of Phoenix, 1991. Profiles more than 100 private and community foundations active in Arizona that have assets over $5,000 and which have made at least $500 in grants. Available from the Junior League of Phoenix, P. O. Box 10377, Phoenix, AZ 85064. Tel: (602) 234-3388.

ARKANSAS Anthes, Earl W., and Jerry Cronin, eds. *The Guide to Arkansas Funding Sources*. 4th ed. West Memphis, AR: Independent Community Consultants, 1990. Contains information on 108 active grantmaking Arkansas foundations, 38 scholarship sources, 5 neighboring foundations (out-of-state foundations with Arkansas giving interests), and 24 religious funding sources. Available from Independent Community Consultants, P. O. Box 141, Hampton, AR 71744. Tel: (501) 798-4510.

CALIFORNIA *Guide to California Foundations*. 8th ed. San Francisco: Northern California Grantmakers, 1991. Lists more than 900 grantmakers located in California awarding grants totaling $40,000 or more annually. Available from Northern California Grantmakers, 116 New Montgomery St., Suite 742, San Francisco, CA 94105. Tel: (415) 777-5761.

CALIFORNIA *Santa Clara County Foundation Directory*. San Jose, CA: Nonprofit Development Center, 1994. Lists foundations that are headquartered in Santa Clara County, or have giving programs there. Available from the Nonprofit Development Center, 1762 Technology Dr., Suite 225, San Jose, CA 95110. Tel: (408) 452-8181.

COLORADO *Colorado Foundation Directory*. 8th ed. Denver, CO: Junior League of Denver, 1992. Information on independent and community foundations, including purpose statement/field of interest, sample grants, and contacts. Available from the Junior League of Denver, 6300 East Yale Ave., Denver, CO 80222. Tel: (303) 692-0270.

COLORADO *Colorado Grants Guide 1993-94*. Denver, CO: Community Resource Center, Inc., 1993. Provides information about public and private sources of nonprofit support in the state of Colorado. Available from the Community Resource Center, 1245 East Colfax Ave., Suite 205, Denver, CO 80218. Tel: (303) 860-7711.

Reprinted by permission from the Guide to U.S. Foundations, Their Trustees, Officers, and Donors. © 1994 by the Foundation Center, 79 Fifth Avenue, New York, NY 10003.

CONNECTICUT Burns, Michael E., ed. *The Connecticut Foundation Directory.* 6th ed. New Haven, CT: Development and Technical Assistance Center, 1990. Provides information on more than 1,250 foundations incorporated in Connecticut. Available from D.A.T.A., 70 Audubon Street, New Haven, CT 06510. Tel: (203) 772-1345.

DELAWARE *Directory of Delaware Grantmakers: 1990.* Wilmington, DE: Delaware Community Foundation, 1990. Biennial directory lists 62 Delaware foundations. Available from the United Way of Delaware, 625 Orange Street, Wilmington, DE 19801. Tel: (302) 573-2414.

DISTRICT OF COLUMBIA *Directory of Foundations of the Greater Washington Area.* Washington: Community Foundation of Greater Washington, 1991. Biennial directory of foundations and trusts located in the greater Washington, D.C., area. Available from the Community Foundation of Greater Washington, 1002 Wisconsin Ave., NW, Washington, DC 20007. Tel: (202) 338-8993.

FLORIDA Culbreath, Alice N., ed. *The Complete Guide to Florida Foundations.* 5th ed. Miami, FL: John L. Adams and Co. (1992). Provides profiles on nearly 1,500 Florida-based foundations. Available from John L. Adams & Co., 9350 South Dixie Highway, Suite 1560, Miami, FL 33156. Tel: (305) 670-2203.

FLORIDA *Foundation Guide: Northeast Florida.* Jacksonville, FL: Volunteer Jacksonville, (1990). Identifies 47 foundations located in Northeast Florida. Available from Volunteer Jacksonville, 1600 Prudential Dr., Jacksonville, FL 32207. Tel: (904) 398-7777.

GEORGIA Sinclair, Ford and Company's *Georgia Foundation Directory* and Service. Atlanta, GA: Sinclair, Ford and Co., 1993. Provides comprehensive profiles of more than 500 foundations located in Georgia, in alphabetical order by name. Geographic index by region and city. Updated quarterly. Available from Sinclair, Ford and Co., 1750 Candler Building, 127 Peachtree St., NE, Atlanta, GA 30303.

HAWAII Hanson, Marcie, comp. *Directory of Charitable Trusts and Foundations for Hawaii's Non-Profit Organizations.* (2nd ed.). Honolulu, HI: Volunteer, Information and Referral Service, 1990. Contains listings for 44 Hawaiian foundations, 10 foundations for individuals in needs, and 27 foundations with a history of grantmaking in Hawaii. Available from Volunteer Information and Referral Service, 200 N. Vineyard, Suite 603, Honolulu, HI 96817. Tel: (808) 536-7234.

IDAHO Leppert, Elaine C., ed. *Directory of Idaho Foundations.* 6th ed. Caldwell, ID: Caldwell Public Library, 1993. Based on 990-PF returns filed with the IRS by foundations and corporations either headquartered in Idaho or with a history of giving in Idaho. Available from the Caldwell Public Library, 1010 Dearborn St., Caldwell, ID 83605-4195. Tel: (208) 459-3242.

ILLINOIS Bowes, Marty, ed. *The Directory of Illinois Foundations.* 2nd ed. Chicago: Donors Forum of Chicago, 1990. Alphabetically arranged directory provides information on 493 Illinois foundations and trusts with assets of $100,000 or more and/or annual grantmaking of at least $25,000. Available from the Donors Forum of Chicago, 53 W. Jackson, Chicago, IL 60604. Tel: (312) 431-0264.

ILLINOIS Dick, Ellen A. *Corporate Foundations in Illinois: A Directory of Illinois Corporate Foundations and Corporate Giving Programs.* 3rd ed. Oak Park, IL: Ellen Dick, 1992. Entries for more than 100 corporate foundations and giving programs. Available from Ellen Dick, 838 Fair Oaks, Oak Park, IL 60302. Tel: (312) 386-9385.

INDIANA Indiana Donors Alliance. *Directory of Indiana Donors.* Indianapolis, IN: Indiana Donors Alliance, 1992. Contains profiles of nearly 800 active grantmaking foundations, trusts, and scholarship programs in Indiana. Available from the Indiana Donors Alliance, 1500 N. Delaware St., Indianapolis, IN 46202. Tel: (317) 638-1500.

IOWA No directory.

KANSAS Rhodes, James H., ed. *The Directory of Kansas Foundations.* 4th ed. Topeka, KS: Topeka and Shawnee County Public Library, 1993. Provides information on approximately 480 foundations and other funding sources. Available from the Topeka and Shawnee County Public Library, Foundation Center Collection, 1515 W. Tenth St., Topeka, KS 66604. Tel: (913) 233-2040.

KENTUCKY *The Kentucky Foundation Directory, 1992.* Cincinnati, OH: MR and Co., 1992. Lists Kentucky foundations with discretionary funds, specific or designated recipients, and terminated or dissolved foundations. Available from MR and Co., P. O. Box 9223, Cincinnati, OH 45209. Tel: (513) 793-4919.

LOUISIANA No directory.

MAINE *Directory of Maine Foundations.* 10th ed. Portland, ME: University of Southern Maine, 1993. Profiles private and community foundations in Maine. Available from the Office of Sponsored Research, University of Southern Maine, 246 Deering Ave., Rm. 628, Portland, ME 04103. Tel: (207) 780-4871.

MARYLAND Maryland Attorney General's Office. *Index of Private Foundations.* Baltimore, MD: Attorney General's Office, 1990. Information on more than 550 foundations compiled from IRS 990-PF forms filed with the Maryland attorney general's office (appendix contains information on 74 foundations that filed after December 1, 1990). Available from the Attorney General's Office, 7 N. Calvert St., Baltimore, MD 21202. Tel: (301) 576-6300.

MASSACHUSETTS Associated Grantmakers of Massachusetts. *Massachusetts Grantmakers.* Boston: Associated Grantmakers of Massachusetts, 1993. Contains descriptions of more than 450 foundations and corporate grantmakers in Massachusetts. Available from Associated Grantmakers of Massachusetts, 294 Washington St., Boston, MA 02108. Tel: (617) 426-2606.

MASSACHUSETTS Peck, Jane, and Charlene Sokal, eds. Worcester County Funding Directory. Worcester, MA: Worcester Public Library, 1991. Profiles more than 160 funders throughout Worcester County. Available from the Worcester Public Library, Grants Resource Center, Salem Square, Worcester, MA 01608. Tel: (508) 799-1655.

MICHIGAN Fischer, Jeri L., ed. *The Michigan Foundation Directory*. 8th ed. Grand Haven, MI: Council of Michigan Foundations, 1992. Identifies more than 1,000 potential grantmaking sources in Michigan. Available from the Council of Michigan Foundations, P. O. Box 599, One South Harbor Ave., Grand Haven, MI 49417. Tel: (616) 842-7080.

MINNESOTA Minnesota Council on Foundations. *Guide to Minnesota Foundations and Corporate Giving Programs: 1993-94*. 7th ed. Minneapolis, MN: Minnesota Council on Foundations, 1993. Lists more than 680 Minnesota grantmakers, while providing full profiles for 340 of them. Available from the Minnesota Council on Foundations, 425 Peavey Building, Minneapolis, MN 55402. Tel: (612) 338-1989.

MISSISSIPPI No directory.

MISSOURI Swift, Wilda H., comp. and ed. *The Directory of Missouri Foundations*. 3rd ed. St. Louis, MO: Swift Associates, 1991. Based on recently filed 990-PF returns and questionnaires of 941 foundations. Available from Swift Associates, 110 Orchard Ave., St. Louis, MO 63119. Tel: (314) 962-2940.

MISSOURI Talbott, Linda Hood, ed. *The Directory of Greater Kansas City Foundations*. Kansas City, MO: Clearinghouse for Midcontinent Foundations, 1990. Profiles 394 foundations and trusts in the eight-county Greater Kansas City (Missouri) metropolitan area. Available from the Clearinghouse for Midcontinent Foundations, P. O. Box 22680, Kansas City, MO 64113-0680. Tel: (816) 235-1176.

MONTANA Grossman, Travis, comp., and JoAnn Meide, ed. *Montana and Wyoming Foundations Directory*. 6th ed. Billings, MT: Eastern Montana College Library, Grants Information Center, 1992. Contains entries for foundations in Montana and Wyoming. Available from the Eastern Montana College Library, 1500 N. 30th St., Billings, MT 59101-0298. Tel: (406) 657-1662.

NEBRASKA No directory.

NEVADA No directory.

NEW HAMPSHIRE No directory.

NEW JERSEY Kay, Linda, comp. *New Jersey Foundations and Other Funding Sources*. (2nd ed.). Trenton, NJ: New Jersey State Library, 1993. This directory is organized into separate alphabetical lists by foundation and county. The listings indicate which reference resources have information about New Jersey private and corporate foundations, corporate giving programs, and some private grantmaking associations. Available from the New Jersey State Library, CN 520, Trenton, NJ 08625-0520. Tel: (908) 292-6220.

NEW JERSEY Littman, Wendy P., ed. *The Mitchell Guide to Foundations, Corporations, and Their Managers*. New Jersey. Belle Mead, NJ: Littman Associates, 1992. Profiles 452 foundations that have made total grants of $15,000 or more annually and/or have assets of $150,000 or more, and provides information on 713 corporations that employ 300 or more New Jersey residents and/or exceed $10 million in sales/revenue. Available from Littman Associates, P. O. Box 613, Belle Mead, NJ 08502. Tel: (609) 359-2215.

NEW MEXICO Wallen, Denise A., ed., and Brian McConnell, asst. ed. *The New Mexico Funding Directory*. 3rd ed. Albuquerque, NM: University of New Mexico, 1993. Contains information on nearly 300 funding sources specific to New Mexico, including private, community, and corporate foundations; state government grant programs; associations and organizations; corporate direct-giving programs; and competitive award programs at the University of New Mexico. Available from the Office of Research Administration, University of New Mexico, Scholes Hall, Room 102, Albuquerque, NM 87131. Tel: (505) 277-2256.

NEW YORK *New York State Foundations: A Comprehensive Directory*. 3rd ed. New York: Foundation Center 1993. A comprehensive directory of the more than 5,000 independent, company-sponsored, and community foundations currently active in New York State that have awarded grants of one dollar or more in the latest fiscal year. Available from the Foundation Center, 79 Fifth Ave., New York, NY 10003-3076. Tel: (800) 424-9836.

NORTH CAROLINA Shirley, Anita Gunn, ed. *North Carolina Giving: The Directory of the State's Foundations*. Raleigh, NC: Capital Consortium, 1993. Based on information taken from 990-PF tax returns filed with the North Carolina Attorney General's Office and the Internal Revenue Service, this directory contains profiles on more than 700 foundations. Available from Capitol Consortium, P. O. Box 2915, Raleigh, NC 27602. Tel: (919) 833-4553.

NORTH DAKOTA No directory.

OHIO *Charitable Foundations Directory of Ohio*. 10th ed. Columbus, OH: Attorney General's Office, 1993. Compiled from the registration forms and annual reports of the approximately 2,000 grantmaking charitable organizations in Ohio, representing $7.4 billion in assets and $534 million in grants. Available from the Attorney General's Office, Charitable Foundations Section, 30 E. Broad St., 15th floor, Columbus, OH 43266-0410. Tel: (614) 466-3180.

OHIO Martindale, Frances R., and Cynthia H. Roy. *The Cincinnati Foundation Directory*. Cincinnati, OH: MR and CO., 1992. Profiles more than 200 foundations and charitable trusts in Cincinnati. Available from MR and Co., P.O. Box 9223, Cincinnati, OH 45209. Tel: (513) 793-4919.

OHIO Martindale, Frances R., and Cynthia H. Roy. *The Southwest Ohio Foundation Directory*. Cincinnati, OH: MR and Co., 1991. Lists approximately 235 foundations and charitable trusts in the southwestern communities of Ohio (excluding Cincinnati). Available from the address above.

OKLAHOMA Streich, Mary Deane, comp. and ed. *The Directory of Oklahoma Foundations*. 4th ed. Oklahoma City, OK: Foundation Research Project, 1992. Based on information from the latest IRS 990-PF forms on file at the state attorney general's office, this directory provides information on Oklahoma foundations. Available from the Foundation Research Project of the Oklahoma City Community Foundation, P. O. Box 1146, Oklahoma City, OK 73101-1146. Tel: (405) 235-5603.

OREGON Smiley, Marc, and Nancy Bridgeford. *Guide to Oregon Foundations*. Portland, OR: United Way of Columbia-Willamette, 1991. Profiles 166 foundations, including those located in Oregon, those with a Northwest regional interest, and those national foundations with a recent history of giving significant amounts to Oregon programs. Available from the United Way of Columbia-Willamette, 718 W. Burnside, Portland, OR 97207. Tel: (503) 226-9348.

PENNSYLVANIA Kletzien, S. Damon, comp. and ed. *Directory of Pennsylvania Foundations*. 4th ed. Springfield, PA: Triadvocates Press, 1990. Based primarily on 990-PF returns filed with the IRS and information supplied by the more than 1,256 foundations listed in the directory. Updated with supplements. Available from Triadvocates Press, P. O. Box 336, Springfield, PA 19064. Tel: (215) 544-6927.

RHODE ISLAND No directory.

SOUTH CAROLINA Williams, Guynell, ed. *South Carolina Foundation Directory*. 4th ed. Columbia, SC: South Carolina State Library, 1990. Based on 990-PF returns filed with the IRS by 288 foundations. Available from the South Carolina State Library, 1500 Senate St., P.O. Box 11469, Columbia, SC 29211. Tel: (803) 734-8666.

SOUTH DAKOTA *The South Dakota Grant Directory*. Pierre, SD: South Dakota State Library, 1992. Contains information on nearly 300 grantmaking institutions in South Dakota, including foundations, state government programs, corporate giving programs, and South Dakota scholarships. Also lists more than 100 major foundations located outside the state that have shown an interest in South Dakota and over 80 non-grantmaking foundations. Available only to South Dakota residents from the South Dakota State Library, 800 Governors Dr., Pierre, SD 57501-2294. Tel: (800) 592-1841 (SD only); (605) 773-5070.

TENNESSEE No directory.

TEXAS Walton, Ed and David Wilkinson, comps. *Directory of Dallas County Foundations, 1990-1991*. 3rd ed. Dallas, TX: Dallas Public Library, 1990. Information on all the private foundations in Dallas County, save those without assets and those recently dissolved, obtained from the foundations' tax returns. Available from the Urban Information Center, Dallas Public Library, 1515 Young St., Dallas, TX 75201. Tel: (214) 670-1487.

TEXAS Walters, Mary Webb, ed. *Directory of Texas Foundations*. 13th ed. San Antonio, TX: Funding Information Center of Texas, 1993. More than 1,700 private and community Texas foundations are profiled. Available from the Funding Information Center of Texas, P. O. Box 15070, San Antonio, TX 78212-8270. Tel: (210) 227-4333.

UTAH Plothow, Roger H., and Lenora D. Plothow. *Philanthropic Foundations of Utah Directory*. 2nd ed. Provo, UT: Henry Dean, 1991. Identifies philanthropic foundations in Utah. Compiled from 1991 IRS 990-PF returns and a survey of foundations listed in the 1989 directory.

VERMONT Graham, Christine, ed. *Vermont Directory of Foundations*. 5th ed. Shaftsbury, VT: CPG Enterprises, 1993. Profiles foundations incorporated in the state of Vermont as well as foundations incorporated outside of Vermont that have demonstrated an interest in funding Vermont nonprofits. Available from CPG Enterprises, Box 199, Shaftsbury, VT 05262. Tel: (802) 447-0256.

VIRGINIA *Directory of Virginia Private Foundations.* Hampton, VA: Hampton Public Library, 1991. Based on IRS 990-PF returns for more than 1,770 foundations. Available from the Reference Department, Hampton Public Library, 4207 Victoria Blvd., Hampton, VA 23669. Tel: (804) 727-1312.

WASHINGTON Moore, Mardell, and Charna Klein. *Washington Foundation Directory: How to Get Your Slice of the Pie.* Seattle, WA: Consultant Services Northwest, 1991. The information included in this directory of some 600 Washington state foundations was culled from IRS 990-PF returns. Available from Consultant Services Northwest, 839 NE 96th St., Seattle, WA 98115. Tel: (206) 524-1950.

WASHINGTON Washington (State). Office of the Attorney General. *Charitable Trust Directory.* Olympia, WA: Attorney General of Washington, 1991. Based on the 1991 records in the files of the attorney general of Washington. Includes information on more than 400 charitable organizations and trusts reporting to the attorney general under the Washington Charitable Trust Act. Available from the Office of the Attorney General, Highways-Licenses Building, 7th floor, Olympia, WA 98504-8071.

WEST VIRGINIA No directory.

WISCONSIN Hopwood, Susan H., ed. *Foundations in Wisconsin: A Directory, 1992.* 11th ed. Milwaukee, WI: Marquette University Memorial Library, 1992. Contains information on 791 active grantmaking foundations. Available from Marquette University Memorial Library, 1415 W. Wisconsin Ave., Milwaukee, WI 53233. Tel: (414) 288-1515.

WYOMING *Wyoming Foundations Directory.* 5th ed. Cheyenne, WY: Laramie County Community College 1992. Divided into two sections: multipurpose foundations and education scholarships/loans. Available from Laramie County Community College Library, 1400 E. College Dr., Cheyenne, WY 82007-3299. Tel: (307) 778-1206.

WYOMING See also MONTANA Grossman, Travis, et al. *The Montana and Wyoming Foundations Directory.*

Appendix B
The Foundation Center

The Foundation Center is an independent national service organization established by foundations to provide an authoritative source of information on private philanthropic giving. In fulfilling its mission, The Foundation Center disseminates information on private giving through public service programs, publications and through a national network of library reference collections for free public use. The New York, Washington, DC, Atlanta, Cleveland and San Francisco reference collections operated by The Foundation Center offer a wide variety of services and comprehensive collections of information on foundations and grants. The Cooperating Collections are libraries, community foundations and other nonprofit agencies that provide a core collection of Foundation Center publications and a variety of supplementary materials and services in subject areas useful to grantseekers.

Many of the network members make available sets of private foundation information returns (IRS Form 990-PF) for their state and/or neighboring states which are available for public use. A complete set of U.S. foundation returns can be found at the New York and Washington, DC, offices of the Foundation Center. The Atlanta, Cleveland, and San Francisco offices contain IRS Form 990-PF returns for the southeastern, midwestern, and western states, respectively.

Those collections marked with a bullet (•) have sets of private foundation returns (IRS Form 990-PF) for their states or regions, available for public reference.

Because the collections vary in their hours, materials and services, IT IS RECOMMENDED THAT YOU CALL EACH COLLECTION IN ADVANCE.

To check on new locations or current information, call toll-free 1-800-424-9836.

Reference Collections
• The Foundation Center
79 Fifth Ave., 8th Fl.
New York, NY 10003
(212) 620-4230
• The Foundation Center
312 Sutter St., Suite 312
San Francisco, CA 94108
(415) 397-0902
• The Foundation Center
1001 Connecticut Ave., N.W.
Washington, DC 20036
(202) 331-1400
• The Foundation Center
Kent H. Smith Library
1422 Euclid, Suite 1356
Cleveland, OH 44115
(216) 861-1933
• The Foundation Center
Suite 150, Grand Lobby
Hurt Building, 50 Hurt Plaza
Atlanta, GA 30303
(404) 880-0094

COOPERATING COLLECTIONS
Alabama
• Birmingham Public Library
Government Documents
2100 Park Place
Birmingham, AL 35203
(205) 226-3600

Huntsville Public Library
915 Monroe Street
Huntsville, AL 35801
(205) 532-5940
• University of South Alabama
Library Building
Mobile, AL 36688
(205) 460-7025
• Auburn University at
Montgomery Library
7300 University Drive
Montgomery, AL 36117
(205) 244-3653
Alaska
• University of Alaska at
Anchorage, Library
3211 Providence Drive
Anchorage, AK 99508
(907) 786-1848
Juneau Public Library
292 Marine Way
Juneau, AK 99801
(907) 586-5267
Arizona
• Phoenix Public Library
Business and Sciences Unit
12 E. McDowell Road
Phoenix, AZ 85004
(602) 262-4636

• Tucson Pima Library
101 N. Stone Avenue
Tucson, AZ 85701
(602) 791-4010
Arkansas
• Westark Community College
Borham Library
5210 Grand Avenue
Fort Smith, AR 72913
(501) 785-7133
• Central Arkansas Library Sys.
700 Louisiana Street
Little Rock, AR 72201
(501) 370-5952
Pine Bluff-Jefferson County
Library System
200 East Eighth
Pine Bluff, AR 71601
(501) 534-2159
California
• Ventura Co. Comm. Foundation
Funding and Information
Resource Center
1355 Del Norte Road
Camarillo, CA 93010
(805) 988-0196
• California Community Foundation
Funding Information Center
606 S. Olive Street, Suite 2400
Los Angeles, CA 90014
(213) 413-4042

Community Foundation for
Monterey County
177 Van Buren
Monterey, CA 93940
(408) 375-9712
Grant and Resource Center of
Northern California
Building C, Suite A
2280 Benton Drive
Redding, CA 96003
(916) 244-1219
Riverside City and County
Public Library
3581 7th Street
Riverside, CA 92502
(714) 782-5201
Nonprofit Resource Center
Sacramento Public Library
828 I Street, 2nd Floor
Sacramento, CA 95812
(916) 552-8817
• San Diego Community Foundation
Funding Information Center
101 W. Broadway, Suite 1120
San Diego, CA 92101
(619) 239-8815
• Nonprofit Development
Center Library
1762 Technology Dr., #225
San Jose, CA 95110
(408) 452-8181
• Peninsula Community Foundation
Funding Information Library
1700 S. El Camino Real, R301
San Mateo, CA 94402
(415) 358-9392
• Volunteer Center of Greater
Orange County
Nonprofit Management Assistance Ctr
1000 E. Santa Ana Blvd., Suite 200
Santa Ana, CA 92701
(714) 953-1655
• Santa Barbara Public Library
40 East Anapamu
Santa Barbara, CA 93101
(805) 962-7653
Santa Monica Public Library
1343 Sixth Street
Santa Monica, CA 90401
(310) 458-8600
Sonoma County Library
3rd & E Streets
Santa Rosa, CA 95404
(707) 545-0831

Colorado
Pikes Peak Library District
20 North Cascade Avenue
Colorado Springs, CO 80901
(719) 531-6333
• Denver Public Library
Social Sciences and Genealogy
1357 Broadway
Denver, CO 80203
(303) 640-8870
Connecticut
Danbury Public Library
170 Main Street
Danbury, CT 06810
(203) 797-4527
• Hartford Public Library
500 Main Street
Hartford, CT 06103
(203) 293-6000
D.A.T.A.
70 Audubon Street
New Haven, CT 06510
(203) 772-1345
Delaware
• University of Delaware
Hugh Morris Library
Newark, DE 19717
(302) 831-2432
District of Columbia
• The Foundation Center
1001 Connecticut Avenue, NW
Washington, DC 20036
(202) 331-1400
Florida
Volusia County Library Center
City Island
Daytona Beach, FL 32014
(904) 255-3765
• Nova University
Einstein Library
3301 College Avenue
Ft. Lauderdale, FL 33314
(305) 475-7050
Indian River Comm. College
Charles S. Miley Learning
Resource Center
3209 Virginia Avenue
Ft. Pierce, FL 34981
(407) 468-4757
• Jacksonville Public Library
Grants Resource Center
122 North Ocean Street
Jacksonville, FL 32202
(904) 630-2665

• Miami-Dade Public Library
Humanities/Social Science
101 W. Flagler Street
Miami, FL 33130
(305) 375-5015
• Orlando Public Library
Social Sciences Department
101 E. Central Blvd.
Orlando, FL 32801
(407) 425-4694
Selby Public Library
1001 Boulevard of the Arts
Sarasota, FL 34236
(813) 951-5501
• Tampa-Hillsborough County
Public Library
900 N. Ashley Drive
Tampa, FL 33602
(813) 273-3628
Community Foundation for
Palm Beach and Martin Counties
324 Datura Street, Suite 340
West Palm Beach, FL 33401
(407) 659-6800
Georgia
• Atlanta-Fulton Public Library
Foundation Collection
Ivan Allen Department
1 Margaret Mitchell Square
Atlanta, GA 30303
(404) 730-1900
• The Foundation Center
Suite 150, Grand Lobby
Hurt Building, 50 Hurt Plaza
Atlanta, GA 30303
(404) 880-0094
Dalton Regional Library
310 Cappes Street
Dalton, GA 30720
(706) 278-4507
Hawaii
• University of Hawaii
Hamilton Library
2550 The Mall
Honolulu, HI 96822
(808) 956-7214
Hawaii Community Foundation
Hawaii Resource Center
222 Merchant Street, 2nd Floor
Honolulu, HI 96813
(808) 537-6333
Idaho
• Boise Public Library
715 S. Capitol Blvd.
Boise, ID 83702
(208) 384-4024

• Caldwell Public Library
1010 Dearborn Street
Caldwell, ID 83605
(208) 459-3242

Illinois
• Donors Forum of Chicago
53 W. Jackson Blvd., #430
Chicago, IL 60604
(312) 431-0265
• Evanston Public Library
1703 Orrington Avenue
Evanston, IL 60201
(708) 866-0305
Rock Island Public Library
401 19th Street
Rock Island, IL 61201
(309) 788-7627
• Sangamon State University
Library
Shepherd Road
Springfield, IL 62794
(217) 786-6633

Indiana
• Allen County Public Library
900 Webster Street
Fort Wayne, IN 46802
(219) 424-0544
Indiana University
Northwest Library
3400 Broadway
Gary, IN 46408
(219) 980-6582
• Indianapolis-Marion County
Public Library
Social Sciences
40 E. St. Clair Street
Indianapolis, IN 46206
(317) 269-1733

Iowa
• Cedar Rapids Public Library
Funding Center Collection
500 First Street, SE
Cedar Rapids, IA 52401
(319) 398-5123
• Southwestern Community
College
Learning Resource Center
1501 W. Townline Road
Creston, IA 50801
(515) 782-7081
• Public Library of Des Moines
100 Locust Street
Des Moines, IA 50309
(515) 283-4152

Kansas
• Topeka and Shawnee County
Public Library
1515 W. Tenth Avenue
Topeka, KS 66604
(913) 233-2040
• Wichita Public Library
223 South Main Street
Wichita, KS 67202
(316) 262-0611

Kentucky
Western Kentucky University
Helm-Cravens Library
Bowling Green, KY 42101
(502) 745-6125
• Louisville Free Public Library
301 York Street
Louisville, KY 40203
(502) 574-1611

Louisiana
• East Baton Rouge Parish Library
Centroplex Branch Grants Collection
120 St. Louis Street
Baton Rouge, LA 70802
(504) 389-4960
Beauregard Parish Library
205 S. Washington Avenue
De Ridder, LA 70634
(318) 463-6217
• New Orleans Public Library
Business and Science Division
219 Loyola Avenue
New Orleans, LA 70140
(504) 596-2580
• Shreve Memorial Library
424 Texas Street
Shreveport, LA 71120
(318) 226-5894

Maine
• University of Southern Maine
Office of Sponsored Research
246 Deering Avenue, Room 628
Portland, ME 04103
(207) 780-4871

Maryland
• Enoch Pratt Free Library
Social Science and History Dept.
400 Cathedral Street
Baltimore, MD 21201
(301) 396-5430

Massachusetts
• Associated Grantmakers
of Massachusetts
Suite 840
294 Washington Street
Boston, MA 02108
(617) 426-2606
• Boston Public Library
Social Science Reference
666 Boylston Street
Boston, MA 02117
(617) 536-5400
Western Mass. Funding
Resource Center
65 Elliot Street
Springfield, MA 01101
(413) 732-3175
• Worcester Public Library
Grants Resource Center
Salem Square
Worcester, MA 01608
(508) 799-1655

Michigan
• Alpena County Library
211 N. First Street
Alpena, MI 49707
(517) 356-6188
• University of Michigan
Graduate Library
Reference & Research Services Dept.
Ann Arbor, MI 48109
(313) 664-9373
• Battle Creek Community Foundation
Southwest Michigan Funding
Resource Center
2 Riverwalk Centre
34 W. Jackson Street
Battle Creek, MI 49017
(616) 962-2181
• Henry Ford Centennial Library
Adult Services
16301 Michigan Avenue
Dearborn, MI 48126
(313) 943-2330
• Wayne State University
Purdy-Kresge Library
5265 Cass Avenue
Detroit, MI 48202
(313) 577-6424
• Michigan State University Libraries
Social Sciences/Humanities
Main Library
East Lansing, MI 48824
(517) 353-8818

137

- Farmington Comm. Library
32737 W. 12 Mile Road
Farmington Hills, MI 48018
(313) 553-0300
- University of Michigan
Flint Library
Flint, MI 48502
(313) 762-3408
- Grand Rapids Public Library
Business Department, 3rd Floor
60 Library Plaza NE
Grand Rapids, MI 49503
(616) 456-3600
- Michigan Technological University
Van Pelt Library
1400 Townsend Drive
Houghton, MI 49931
(906) 487-2507
Sault Ste. Marie Area
Public Schools
Office of Compensatory Education
460 W. Spruce Street
Sault Ste. Marie, MI 49783
(906) 635-6619
- Northwestern Michigan College
Mark & Helen Osterin Library
1701 E. Front Street
Traverse City, MI 49684
(616) 922-1060

Minnesota
- Duluth Public Library
520 W. Superior Street
Duluth, MN 55802
(218) 723-3802
Southwest State University
University Library
Marshall, MN 56258
(507) 537-6176
- Minneapolis Public Library
Sociology Department
300 Nicollet Mall
Minneapolis, MN 55401
(612) 372-6555
Rochester Public Library
11 First Street, SE
Rochester, MN 55904
(507) 285-8002
Saint Paul Public Library
90 W. Fourth Street
Saint Paul, MN 55102
(612) 292-6307

Mississippi
- Jackson/Hinds Library System
300 N. State Street
Jackson, MS 39201
(601) 968-5803

Missouri
- Clearinghouse for Midcontinent
Foundations
University of Missouri
5315 Rockhill Road
Kansas City, MO 64110
(816) 235-1176
- Kansas City Public Library
311 E. 12th Street
Kansas City, MO 64106
(816) 235-9650
- Metropolitan Association for
Philanthropy, Inc.
5615 Pershing Avenue, Suite 20
St. Louis, MO 63112
(314) 361-3900
- Springfield-Greene Co. Library
397 E. Central Street
Springfield, MO 65802
(417) 869-9400

Montana
- Eastern Montana College Library
Special Collections-Grants
1500 N. 30th Street
Billings, MT 59101
(406) 657-1662
Bozeman Public Library
220 E. Lamme
Bozeman, MT 59715
(406) 586-4787
- Montana State Library
Library Services
1515 E. 6th Avenue
Helena, MT 59620
(406) 444-3004

Nebraska
- University of Nebraska
Love Library
14th and R Streets
Lincoln, NE 68588
(402) 472-2848
- W. Dale Clark Library
Social Sciences Department
215 S. 15th Street
Omaha, NE 68102
(402) 444-4826

Nevada
- Las Vegas-Clark County
Library District
833 Las Vegas Blvd. North
Las Vegas, NV 89101
(702) 382-5280
- Washoe County Library
301 S. Center Street
Reno, NV 89501
(702) 785-4010

New Hampshire
- New Hampshire Charitable Fund
One South Street
Concord, NH 03302
(603) 225-6641
- Plymouth State College
Herbert H. Lamson Library
Plymouth, NH 03264
(603) 535-2258

New Jersey
Cumberland County Library
New Jersey Room
800 E. Commerce Street
Bridgeton, NJ 08302
(609) 453-2210
- Free Public Library of Elizabeth
11 S. Broad Street
Elizabeth, NJ 07202
(908) 354-6060
County College of Morris
Learning Resource Center
214 Center Grove Road
Randolph, NJ 07869
(201) 328-5296
- New Jersey State Library
Governmental Reference Services
185 W. State Street
Trenton, NJ 08625
(609) 292-6220

New Mexico
Albuquerque Community Foundation
3301 Menual N.E., Suite 16
Albuquerque, NM 87176
(505) 883-6240
- New Mexico State Library
Information Services
325 Don Gaspar
Santa Fe, NM 87503
(505) 827-3824

New York
- New York State Library
Humanities Reference
Cultural Education Center
Empire State Plaza
Albany, NY 12230
(518) 474-5355
Suffolk Coop Library System
627 N. Sunrise Service Road
Bellport, NY 11713
(516) 286-1600
New York Public Library
Fordham Branch
2556 Bainbridge Avenue
Bronx, NY 10458
(212) 220-6575

Brooklyn-In-Touch Information Ctr.
Room 2504
One Hanson Place
Brooklyn, NY 11243
(718) 230-3200
• Buffalo and Erie County
Public Library
History Department
Lafayette Square
Buffalo, NY 14203
(716) 858-7103
Huntington Public Library
338 Main Street
Huntington, NY 11743
(516) 427-5165
Queens Borough Public Library
Social Sciences Division
89-11 Merrick Blvd.
Jamaica, NY 11432
(718) 990-0700
• Levittown Public Library
One Bluegrass Lane
Levittown, NY 11756
(516) 731-5728
New York Public Library
Countee Cullen Branch Library
104 West 136th Street
New York, NY 10030
(212) 491-2070
• The Foundation Center
79 Fifth Avenue
New York, NY 10003
(212) 620-4230
Adriance Memorial Library
Special Services Department
93 Market Street
Poughkeepsie, NY 12601
(914) 485-3445
• Rochester Public Library
Business, Economics and Law
115 South Avenue
Rochester, NY 14604
(716) 428-7328
Onondaga Co. Public Library
447 S. Salina Street
Syracuse, NY 13202
(315) 448-4700
Utica Public Library
303 Genesee Street
Utica, NY 13501
(315) 735-2279

• White Plains Public Library
100 Martine Avenue
White Plains, NY 10601
(914) 442-1480
North Carolina
• Asheville-Buncombe Technical
Community College
Learning Resources Center
14 College Street
P.O. Box 1888
Asheville, NC 28801
(704) 254-4960
• The Duke Endowment
200 S. Tryon Street, #1100
Charlotte, NC 28202
(704) 376-0291
Durham County Public Library
301 N. Roxboro Street
Durham, NC 27702
(919) 560-0110
• State Library of North Carolina
Government and Business Services
Archives Building
109 E. Jones Street
Raleigh, NC 27601
(919) 733-3270
• The Winston-Salem Foundation
310 W. 4th Street, Suite 229
Winston-Salem, NC 27101
(919) 725-2382
North Dakota
• North Dakota State University
The Library
Fargo, ND 58105
(701) 237-8886
Ohio
Stark County District Library
Humanities
715 Market Avenue North
Canton, OH 44702
(216) 452-0665
• Public Library of Cincinnati
and Hamilton County
Grants Resource Center
800 Vine Street-Library Square
Cincinnati, OH 45202
(513) 369-6940
• The Foundation Center
Kent H. Smith Library
1442 Euclid Building, Suite 1356
Cleveland, OH 44115
(216) 861-1933

Columbus Metro. Library
Business and Technology
96 S. Grant Ave.
Columbus, OH 43215
(614) 645-2590
• Dayton and Montgomery County
Public Library
215 E. Third Street
Dayton, OH 45402
(513) 227-9500 ext. 211
• Toledo-Lucas County
Public Library
Social Science Department
325 Michigan Street
Toledo, OH 43624
(419) 259-5245
Youngstown & Mahoning
County Library
305 Wick Avenue
Youngstown, OH 44503
(216) 744-8636
Muskinghum County Library
220 N. 5th Street
Zanesville, OH 43701
(614) 453-0391
Oklahoma
• Oklahoma City University
Dulaney Browne Library
2501 N. Blackwelder
Oklahoma City, OK 73106
(405) 521-5072
• Tulsa City-Co. Library System
400 Civic Center
Tulsa, OK 74103
(918) 596-7944
Oregon
Oregon Inst of Technology Library
3201 Campus Drive
Klamath Falls, OR 97601
(503) 885-1773
Pacific Non-Profit Network
Grantsmanship Resource Library
33 N. Central, Suite 211
Medford, OR 97501
(503) 779-6044
• Multnomah County Library
Government Documents
801 S.W. Tenth Avenue
Portland, OR 97205
(503) 248-5123
Oregon State Library
State Library Building
Salem, OR 97310
(503) 378-4277

Pennsylvania
Northampton Community College
Learning Resources Center
3835 Green Pond Road
Bethlehem, PA 18017
(215) 861-5360
Erie County Library System
27 S. Park Row
Erie, PA 16501
(814) 451-6927
Dauphin County Library System
Central Library
101 Walnut Street
Harrisburg, PA 17101
(717) 234-4961
Lancaster County Public Library
125 N. Duke Street
Lancaster, PA 17602
(717) 394-2651
• Free Library of Philadelphia
Regional Foundation Center
Logan Square
Philadelphia, PA 19103
(215) 686-5423
• Carnegie Library of Pittsburgh
Foundation Collection
4400 Forbes Avenue
Pittsburgh, PA 15213
(412) 622-1917
Pocono Northeast Development Fund
James Pettinger Memorial Library
1151 Oak Street
Pittston, PA 18640
(717) 655-5581
Reading Public Library
100 S. Fifth Street
Reading, PA 19602
(215) 655-6355
Martin Library
159 Market Street
York, PA 17401
(717) 846-5300

Rhode Island
• Providence Public Library
150 Empire Street
Providence, RI 02906
(401) 521-7722

South Carolina
• Charleston County Library
404 King Street
Charleston, SC 29403
(803) 723-1645
• South Carolina State Library
1500 Senate Street
Columbia, SC 29211
(803) 734-8666

South Dakota
Nonprofit Grants Assistance Center
Business and Education Institute
Washington Street, East Hall
Dakota State University
Madison, SD 57042
(605) 256-5555
• South Dakota State Library
800 Governors Drive
Pierre, SD 57501
(605) 773-5070
(800) 592-1841 (SD residents)
Sioux Falls Area Foundation
141 N. Main Ave., Suite 310
Sioux Falls, SD 57102
(605) 336-7055

Tennessee
• Knox County Public Library
500 W. Church Avenue
Knoxville, TN 37902
(615) 544-5700
• Memphis & Shelby County
Public Library
1850 Peabody Avenue
Memphis, TN 38104
(901) 725-8877
• Nashville Public Library
Business Information Division
225 Polk Avenue
Nashville, TN 37203
(615) 862-5843

Texas
Community Foundation of Abilene
Funding Information Library
500 N. Chestnut, Suite 1509
Abilene, TX 79604
(915) 676-3883
• Amarillo Area Foundation
700 First National Place
801 S. Fillmore
Amarillo, TX 79101
(806) 376-4521
• Hogg Foundation for
Mental Health
Will C. Hogg Building, Suite 301
Inner Campus Drive
University of Texas
Austin, TX 78713
(512) 471-5041
Texas A & M University
Library-Reference Dept.
6300 Ocean Drive
Corpus Christi, TX 78412
(512) 994-2608

• Dallas Public Library
Urban Information
1515 Young Street
Dallas, TX 75201
(214) 670-1487
El Paso Community Foundation
1616 Texas Commerce Building
El Paso, TX 79901
(915) 533-4020
• Funding Information Center
Texas Christian University Library
2800 S. University Drive
Ft. Worth, TX 76129
(817) 921-7664
• Houston Public Library
Bibliographic Information Center
500 McKinney Avenue
Houston, TX 77002
(713) 236-1313
• Longview Public Library
222 W. Cotton Street
Longview, TX 75601
(903) 237-1352
Lubbock Area Foundation
502 Texas Commerce Bank Bldg.
Lubbock, TX 79401
(806) 762-8061
• Funding Information Center
530 McCullough, Suite 600
San Antonio, TX 78212
(210) 227-4333
North Texas Center for
Nonprofit Management
624 Indiana, Suite 307
Wichita Falls, TX 76301
(817) 322-4961

Utah
• Salt Lake City Public Library
209 E. 500 South
Salt Lake City, UT 84111
(801) 524-8200

Vermont
• Vermont Department of Libraries
Reference & Law Info. Services
109 State Street
Montpelier, VT 05609
(802) 828-3268

Virginia
• Hampton Public Library
4207 Victoria Blvd.
Hampton, VA 23669
(804) 727-1312

- Richmond Public Library
Business, Science & Technology Department
101 E. Franklin Street
Richmond, VA 23219
(804) 780-8223
- Roanoke City Public Library System
Central Library
706 S. Jefferson Street
Roanoke, VA 24016
(703) 981-2477

Washington
- Mid-Columbia Library
405 S. Dayton
Kennewick, WA 99336
(509) 586-3156
- Seattle Public Library
Science, Social Science
1000 Fourth Avenue
Seattle, WA 98104
(206) 386-4620
- Spokane Public Library
Funding Information Center
West 811 Main Avenue
Spokane, WA 99201
(509) 838-3364
- United Way of Pierce County
Center for Nonprofit Development
734 Broadway
P.O. Box 2215
Tacoma, WA 98401
(206) 597-6686
Greater Wenatchee Community Foundation at the Wenatchee Public Library
310 Douglas Street
Wenatchee, WA 98807
(509) 662-5021

West Virginia
- Kanawha County Public Library
123 Capital Street
Charleston, WV 25301
(304) 343-4646

Wisconsin
- University of Wisconsin
Memorial Library
728 State Street
Madison, WI 53706
(608) 262-3242
- Marquette University
Memorial Library
Funding Information Center
1415 W. Wisconsin Avenue
Milwaukee, WI 53233
(414) 288-1515

Wyoming
- Natrona County Public Library
307 East 2nd Street
Casper, WY 82601
(307) 237-4935
- Laramie Co. Community College
Instructional Resource Center
1400 E. College Drive
Cheyenne, WY 82007
(307) 778-1206
- Campbell County Public Library
2101 4-J Road
Gillette, WY 82716
(307) 682-3223
- Teton County Library
320 South King Street
Jackson, WY 83001
(307) 733-2164
Rock Springs Library
400 C Street
Rock Springs, WY 82901
(307) 362-6212

Puerto Rico
University of Puerto Rico
Ponce Technological College Library
Box 7186
Ponce, PR 00732
(809) 844-8181
Universidad Del Sagrado Corazon
M.M.T. Guevara Library
Santurce, PR 00914
(809) 728-1515 ext. 357

Appendix C

The Grantsmanship Center

The Grantsmanship Center is the world's oldest and largest training organization for the nonprofit sector. Since it was founded in 1972, the Center has trained more than 60,000 staff members of public and private agencies in grantsmanship, program management and fundraising.

The five-day Grantsmanship Training Program, first offered in 1972 and continuously updated, began a new era in training seminars and workshops for nonprofit agencies. Over 30,000 nonprofit agency staff members have attended this demanding, week-long workshop, the single most widely attended training program in the history of the nonprofit sector. It covers all aspects of researching for grants, writing grant proposals, and negotiating with funding sources.

The Grant Proposal Writing Workshop, an intensive three-day laboratory, teaches you how to write a good proposal and plan better programs at the same time, using the Grantsmanship Center's program planning and proposal writing format.

The Center also produces publications on grantsmanship, planning, fundraising, management, and personnel issues for nonprofit agencies. Its Program Planning and Proposal Writing booklet is now a classic in the field and has been used by hundreds of thousands of successful grant seekers.

For detailed information about The Grantsmanship Center's training programs, publications, and other services to the nonprofit sector, write to The Grantsmanship Center, Dept. DD, P.O. Box 17220, Los Angeles, CA 90017 and ask for a free copy of *The Grantsmanship Center Magazine*.

Index to Foundations

(Alphabetical)

Citations are by entry number

A

Abell (Charles S.) Foundation, Inc., 249

Abell-Hanger Foundation, 586

Abercrombie Foundation, 587

Abreu (Francis L.) Charitable Trust u/w of May P. Abreu, 122

Achelis Foundation, 406

AHS Foundation, 324

Air Products Foundation, 527

Alabama Power Foundation, Inc., 1

Alaska Conservation Foundation, 7

Albers (William H.) Foundation, Inc., 473

Alcoa Foundation, 528

Alexander (Judd S.) Foundation, Inc., 656

Alexander (Saul) Foundation, 569

AlliedSignal Foundation, 394

American Conservation Association, 407

American Financial Corporation Foundation, 474

American Honda Foundation, 17

American National Bank and Trust Company of Chicago Foundation, 154

Amini Foundation, 588

Amoco Foundation, Inc., 155

Anderson (John W.) Foundation, 195

ANR Foundation, Inc., 284

Anschutz Family Foundation, 70

Anthony (Barbara Cox) Foundation, 141

AON Foundation, 156

Arcadia Foundation, 529

ARCO Foundation, 18

Arizona Community Foundation, 8

Ashbrook (Mary K.) Foundation for El Reno, Oklahoma, 513

AT&T Foundation, 408

Atherton Family Foundation, 142

Athwin Foundation, 325

Atkinson Foundation, 19

Ayres Foundation, Inc., 196

B

Babcock (Mary Reynolds) Foundation, Inc., 458

Badger Meter Foundation, Inc., 657

Baer (Alan and Marcia) Foundation, 383

Baker Foundation, 326

Baker (Solomon R. & Rebecca D.) Fdn., 20

Baldwin (Theodore G.) Foundation, 384

Ball Brothers Foundation, 197

Bamberger (Ruth Eleanor) and John Ernest Bamberger Memorial Foundation, 630

Bank IV Charitable Trust, 220

Barker (Donald R.) Foundation, 21

Barstow Foundation, 285

Battle Creek Community Foundation, 286

Bauervic-Paisley Foundation, 287

Baughman Foundation, 221

Baumker (Elsie and Harry) Charitable Fdn., 475

Bayrd (Adelaide Breed) Foundation, 256

Beazley Foundation, Inc., 635

Beckman (Leland D.) Foundation, 149

Bedsole (J.L.) Foundation, 2

Belk Foundation, 459

Bell & Howell Foundation, 157

Benedum (Claude Worthington) Foundation, 530

Bersted Foundation, 158

Besser Foundation, 288

Bettingen (Burton G.) Corporation, 22

Bicknell Fund, 476

Bingham (William) Foundation, 477

Bishop (A.G.) Charitable Trust, 289

Bitner (H.M.) Charitable Trust, 531

Blaffer (Robert Lee) Trust, 198

Block (H & R) Foundation, 362

Blowitz-Ridgeway Foundation, 159

Bodman Foundation, 409

Boettcher Foundation, 71

Borden Foundation, Inc., 478

Borkee-Hagley Foundation, Inc., 91

Boston Edison Foundation, 257

Boston Globe Foundation II, Inc., 258

Brach (Helen) Foundation, 160

Braden (Clifford) Foundation, 643

Bremer (Otto) Foundation, 327

Bright (Alexander H.) Charitable Trust, 259

Brown (Alex) and Sons Charitable Fdn., 250

Brown Foundation, Inc., 589

Brown Group, Inc. Charitable Trust, 363

Brown (H.L. & Elizabeth M.) Foundation, 590

Brown (Joe W. and Dorothy Dorsett) Fdn., 239

Brunswick Foundation, Inc., 161

Bryan (Kathleen Price and Joseph M.) Family Foundation, 460

BT Foundation, 410

Bucyrus-Erie Foundation, Inc., 658

Buffalo Foundation, 411

Bullitt Foundation, Inc., 644

Burkitt Foundation, 591

Bush (Edyth) Charitable Foundation, Inc., 105

Butz Foundation, 162

C

Cafritz (Morris and Gwendolyn) Foundation, 95

Cain (Effie & Wofford) Foundation, 592

Cain (Gordon and Mary) Foundation, 593

Calder (Louis) Foundation, 412

Callaway (Fuller E.) Foundation, 123

Camp (Samuel Higby) Foundation, 290

Campbell (Bushrod H.) and Adah F. Hall Charity Fund, 260

Canaan Foundation for Christian Education, 633

Carey (Charles E.) Foundation, Inc., 222

Cargill Foundation, 328

Carpenter Foundation, 521

Carstensen (Fred R. & Hazel W.) Memorial Foundation, Inc., 85

Castle Foundation, 631

Cemala Foundation, Inc., 461

Centerior Energy Foundation, 479

Chamberlain Foundation, 72

Chamberlin (Clarence and Grace) Foundation, 291

Chase Manhattan Foundation, 413

Chatam, Inc., 391

Chatlos Foundation, Inc., 106

Cheney (Ben B.) Foundation, Inc., 645

Chicago Community Trust, 163

Chichester duPont Foundation, Inc., 92

Childs (Roberta M.) Charitable Foundation, 261

Chope Foundation, Inc., 480

CIGNA Foundation, 532

Clark Charitable Trust, 262

Clark Foundation, 414

Clayton Fund, Inc., 594

Cleveland Foundation, 481

Clipper Ship Foundation, Inc., 263

Clorox Company Foundation, 23

Clowes Fund, Inc., 199

Coca-Cola Foundation, Inc., 124

Cochener (Bruce G.) Foundation, 223

Cockrell Foundation, 595

Cole (Olive B.) Foundation, Inc., 200

Coleman Foundation, Inc., 164

Collins Foundation, 73

Columbia Foundation, 251

Columbus Foundation, 482

Community Foundation of Abilene, 596

Community Foundation of Greater New Haven, 86

Community Foundation of Henderson Co., 462

Community Foundation for Monterey County, 24

Community Foundation for Northeast Michigan, 292

Community Foundation of Shreveport-Bossier, 240

Community Foundation for Southeastern Michigan, 293

Compton Foundation, Inc., 25

Conn Memorial Foundation, Inc., 107

Connecticut Mutual Life Foundation, Inc., 87

Consolidated Natural Gas Company Fdn., 533

Cooke Foundation, Limited, 143

Cooley (Denton A.) Foundation, 597

Coonley (Queene Ferry) Foundation, Inc., 96

Coors (Adolph) Foundation, 74

Cornell (Peter C.) Trust, 415

Cowan (Lillian L. and Harry A.) Foundation Corporation, 264

Cowles Charitable Trust, 416

Cowles (Gardner and Florence Call) Fdn., 216

CPI Corporation Philanthropic Trust, 364

Cranston Foundation, 566

Cray Research Foundation, 329

Crestlea Foundation, Inc., 93

Cudahy (Patrick and Anna M.) Fund, 659

CUNA Mutual Insurance Group Charitable Foundation, Inc., 660

D

Dalton (Dorothy U.) Foundation, Inc., 294

Dana Corporation Foundation, 483

Daniels (Fred Harris) Foundation, Inc., 265

Dater (Charles H.) Foundation, Inc., 484
Davenport (George P.) Trust Fund, 246
Davis (Edwin W. and Catherine M.) Fdn., 330
Day (Doris and Victor) Foundation, Inc., 165
Dayton Hudson Foundation, 331
Dayton Power & Light Company Foundation, 485
De Queen General Hospital Foundation, Inc., 13
Deluxe Corporation Foundation, 332
Deposit Guaranty Foundation, 359
DeRoy (Helen L.) Foundation, 295
Detroit Edison Foundation, 296
DeVore Foundation, Inc., 224
Diamond (Aaron) Foundation, Inc., 417
Dickson (Raymond) Foundation, 598
Dietrich (William B.) Foundation, 534
Doherty, Rumble & Butler Foundation, 333
Dolfinger-McMahon Foundation, 535
Donnelley (Gaylord and Dorothy) Foundation, 166
Doolittle (Elizabeth Elser) Charitable Trust No. 1, 661
Dorr Foundation, 418
Dorset Foundation, Inc., 599
Dougherty, Jr. (James R.) Foundation, 600
Dow (Alden & Vada) Fund, 297
Drown (Joseph) Foundation, 26
Dufresne Foundation, 382
Duke Endowment, 463
Duluth-Superior Area Community Foundation, 334
Dunn (Robert and Polly) Foundation, Inc., 125

E

Eaton Charitable Fund, 486
Eberbach (Carl and Elisabeth) Foundation, Inc., 662
Eccles (Marriner S.) Foundation, 632
Eckerd (Jack) Corporation Foundation, 108
Eden Foundation, 536
Edwards (J.E.S.) Foundation, 601
El Pomar Foundation, 75
Ellsworth (Ruth H. and Warren A.) Foundation, 266
Ellwood Foundation, 602
Enron Foundation, 603
Evanston Community Foundation, 167
Evinrude (Ralph) Foundation, Inc., 663

F

Falk (David) Foundation, Inc., 109
Favrot Foundation, 604

Feld (Milton W.) Charitable Trust, 365
Ferguson (Roger and Sybil) Charitable Fdn., 150
Fibre Converters Foundation, Inc., 298
Field Foundation of Illinois, Inc., 168
1525 Foundation, 487
Fikes (Leland) Foundation, Inc., 605
Fink Foundation, 225
Finley (A.E.) Foundation, Inc., 464
First Bank System Foundation, 335
First Interstate Bank of California Foundation, 27
First Interstate Bank of Nevada Foundation, 388
First Interstate Foundation of Texas, 606
First Mississippi Corporation Foundation, Inc., 360
First National Bank of Chicago Foundation, 169
Fleishhacker Foundation, 28
Fleming Foundation, 607
Flintridge Foundation, 29
Fluor Foundation, 30
Foellinger Foundation, 201
Ford Meter Box Foundation, Inc., 202
Forest Foundation, 646
Forest Fund, 170
Foundation of the Litton Industries, 31
Foundation for the Tri-State Community, Inc., 233
Fowler (John Edward) Memorial Foundation, 97
Fraser (Isobel A.) & Nancy F. Parker Charitable Trust, 126
Frazier Foundation, Inc., 241
Frear (Mary D. and Walter F.) Eleemosynary Trust, 144
Freed Foundation, 98
Freedom Forum, 636
Fremont Area Foundation, 299
Froderman Foundation, Inc., 203
Frueauff (Charles A.) Foundation, Inc., 110
Fullerton Foundation, 570

G

Gabelli Foundation, Inc., 389
Gap Foundation, 32
Gardner Foundation, 664
Garvey (Olive White) Trust, 226
Gault-Hussey Charitable Trust, 227
Gebbie Foundation, Inc., 419
Gellert (Carl) Foundation, 33
Gellert (Celia Berta) Foundation, 34
Gellert (Fred) Foundation, 35

General Mills Foundation, 336
General Motors Foundation, Inc., 300
George Foundation, 608
Georgia Power Foundation, Inc., 127
Gifford (Rosamond) Charitable Corporation, 420
Gilmore (Irving S.) Foundation, 301
Glaxo Foundation, 465
Gleason Memorial Fund, Inc., 421
Glick (Eugene and Marilyn) Foundation Corporation, 204
Goddard (Charles B.) Foundation, 514
Grable Foundation, 537
Grace Foundation, Inc., 111
Graco Foundation, 337
Grand Metropolitan Food Sector Foundation, 338
Greater Kanawha Valley Foundation, 654
Greater Santa Cruz County Community Fdn., 36
Greater Tacoma Community Foundation, 647
Green (Ralph & Sylvia G.) Charitable Fdn., 217
Greystone Foundation, 339
Griggs (Mary Livingston) and Mary Griggs Burke Foundation, 340
Grundy Foundation, 538
Gumbiner (Josephine S.) Foundation, 37
Gund (George) Foundation, 488

H

Haas (Paul and Mary) Foundation, 609
Haas (Walter and Elise) Fund, 38
Hagedorn Fund, 422
Hallmark Corporate Foundation, 366
Halsell (Ewing) Foundation, 610
Hamrick Mills Foundation, Inc., 571
Hancock (Luke B.) Foundation, 39
Hansen (Dane G.) Foundation, 228
Harden Foundation, 40
Hardin (Phil) Foundation, 361
Hargis (Estes H. and Florence Parker) Charitable Foundation, 3
Harland (John H. and Wilhelmina D.) Charitable Foundation, Inc., 128
Harriman (Mary W.) Trust, 423
Harrington (Francis A. & Jacquelyn H.) Fdn., 267
Harris Bank Foundation, 171
Harris Foundation, 172
Harris Foundation, Inc., 515
Hawaii Community Foundation, 145
HCA Foundation, 577

Hearst Foundation, Inc., 424
Heinz (Vira I.) Endowment, 539
Helmerich Foundation, 516
Heritage Fund of Bartholomew County, 205
Hermann (Grover) Foundation, 173
Hewlett (William and Flora) Foundation, 41
Hill (Walter Clay) and Family Foundation, 129
Hill Crest Foundation, Inc., 4
Hillman (Henry L.) Foundation, 540
Hilton (Conrad N.) Foundation, 390
Holden (James and Lynelle) Fund, 302
Hollis (William M. & Nina B.) Foundation, 112
Honeywell Foundation, 341
Hoover Foundation, 489
Houston Endowment, Inc., 611
Howe (Lucile Horton) and Mitchell B. Howe Foundation, 42
Hoyt (Stewart W. & Willma C.) Foundation, 425
Hudson-Webber Foundation, 303
Huie-Dellmon Trust, 242
Humphrey (George M. and Pamela S.) Fund, 490
Humphreys Foundation, 76
Hunter (A. V.) Trust, Inc., 77
Hurst Foundation, 304
Hyams Foundation, 268

I

Idaho Community Foundation, 151
Iddings Foundation, 491
Imperial Foundation, 385
Indianapolis Foundation, 206
International Multifoods Charitable Fdn., 342
Island Foundation, Inc., 269

J

Jackson Community Foundation, 305
Jacobs Family Foundation, Inc., 43
Jenkins (George W.) Foundation, Inc., 113
Jewett (George Frederick) Foundation, 44
Joanna Foundation, 572
Johnson & Johnson Family of Companies Contribution Fund, 395
Johnson (Christian A.) Endeavor Foundation, 426
Johnson (Helen K. and Arthur E.) Foundation, 78
Johnson (Samuel S.) Foundation, 522
Jones (Cyrus W. & Amy F.) & Bessie D. Phelps Foundation, Inc., 88

Jones (Daisy Marquis) Foundation, 427
Jordan (Arthur) Foundation, 207
Joslyn (Carl W. and Carrie Mae) Charitable Trust, 79
Jost (Charles and Mabel P.) Foundation, 89
Jostens Foundation, Inc., 343
Journal Gazette Foundation, Inc., 208
Joy Family Foundation, 428
Joyce Foundation, 174

K

Kalamazoo Foundation, 306
Kaufman (Louis G.) Endowment Fund, 307
Kavanagh (T. James) Foundation, 541
Kayser-Roth Hosiery Charitable Foundation, 466
Keith (Ben E.) Foundation Trust, 612
Kempner (Harris and Eliza) Fund, 613
Kennedy, Jr. (Joseph P.) Foundation, 99
Kettering Family Foundation, 492
Kieckhefer (J.W.) Foundation, 9
Kimberly-Clark Foundation, Inc., 614
Kiplinger Foundation, 100
Kirchgessner (Karl) Foundation, 45
Kirkpatrick Foundation, Inc., 517
Knight (John S. and James L.) Foundation, 114
Knott (Marion I. and Henry J.) Foundation, 25
Koehler (Marcia and Otto) Foundation, 615
Komes Foundation, 46
Koret Foundation, 47
Kramer (Charles G. and Rheta) Foundation, 175
Krause (Henry) Charitable Foundation, 229

L

Laclede Gas Charitable Trust, 367
Lang (Eugene M.) Foundation, 429
Laurel Foundation, 542
Leach (Tom and Frances) Foundation, Inc., 470
Lee (Ray M. and Mary Elizabeth) Foundation, 130
LGH Foundation, Inc., 209
Lied Foundation Trust, 386
Lilly (Eli) and Company Foundation, 210
Lilly Endowment Inc., 211
Lindsay (Agnes M.) Trust, 392
Little (Arthur D.) Foundation, 270
Long (R.A.) Foundation, 368
Louisville Community Foundation, Inc., 234

Lowenstein (William P. and Marie R.) Fdn., 578
LTV Foundation Charitable and Educational Trust, 493
Lubrizol Foundation, 494
Lupin Foundation, 243
Lurie (Louis R.) Foundation, 48
Lyndhurst Foundation, 579
Lyon Foundation, Inc., 308
Lytel (Bertha Ross) Foundation, 49

M

MacArthur (John D. and Catherine T.) Fdn., 176
Macdonald (James A.) Foundation, 430
Maclellan Foundation, Inc., 580
Maclellan (R.J.) Charitable Trust, 581
Madison Community Foundation, 665
MAHADH Foundation, 344
Maier (Sarah and Pauline) Foundation, Inc., 655
Maneely Fund, Inc., 396
Marin Community Foundation, 50
Marley Fund, 230
Marshall (Mattie H.) Foundation, 131
Material Service Foundation, 177
Mather (Elizabeth Ring) and William Gwinn Mather Fund, 495
Mather (S. Livingston) Charitable Trust, 496
Matlock Foundation, 648
Mattel Foundation, 51
Mauldin Foundation, Inc., 132
Maytag (Fred) Family Foundation, 218
McBeath (Faye) Foundation, 666
McCormick (Robert R.) Tribune Foundation, 178
McDermott (Eugene) Foundation, 616
McGee Foundation, 369
McGraw Foundation, 179
McGraw-Hill Foundation, Inc., 431
McGregor Fund, 309
McInerny Foundation, 146
McIntosh (Alex & Agnes O.) Foundation, 115
MCJ Foundation, 432
McKee (Robert E. and Evelyn) Foundation, 617
McKesson Foundation, Inc., 52
McKnight (Loretta Haley) Charitable Trust Fund, 133
McKnight Foundation, 345
Meadows Foundation, Inc., 618
Medina Foundation, 649
Medtronic Foundation, 346

Mellon Bank Foundation, 543
Mellon (R.K.) Family Foundation, 544
Mellon (Richard King) Foundation, 545
Memorial Foundation for Children, 637
Merrill Lynch & Company Foundation, Inc., 433
Metcalf (Stanley W.) Foundation, Inc., 434
Metropolitan Atlanta Community Fdn., Inc., 134
Meyer (Eugene and Agnes E.) Foundation, 101
Meyer Memorial Trust, 523
Mid-Iowa Health Foundation, 219
Mills (Frances Goll) Fund, 310
Minneapolis Foundation, 347
Minnesota Mining and Manufacturing Fdn., 348
Moerlein (Charles) Foundation, 497
Morgan (J. P.) Charitable Trust, 435
Morgan-Worcester, Inc., 271
Morley Brothers Foundation, 311
Morris (Margaret T.) Foundation, 10
Morrison (Harry W.) Foundation, Inc., 152
Moses (Henry and Lucy) Fund, Inc., 436
Mosher (Samuel B.) Foundation, 53
Moss (Finis M.) Charitable Trust, 370
Moss (Harry S.) Heart Trust, 619
Mulcahy Foundation, 11
Murphy Foundation, 14
Murphy (John P.) Foundation, 498
Murphy (Katherine John) Foundation, 135
Muskegon County Community Foundation, 312
Myers Foundation, Inc., 349

N

Nalco Foundation, 180
Nationwide Insurance Foundation, 499
Needmor Fund, 80
Nelson (Grace S. and W. Linton) Foundation, 546
Nettelroth (Herman H.) Fund, 235
New Hampshire Ball Bearings Foundation, 393
New Horizon Foundation, 650
New Street Foundation, Inc., 437
New York Life Foundation, 438
Nolan (William C. and Theodosia Murphy) Foundation, 15
Norcliffe Foundation, 651
Norfolk Southern Foundation, 638
North Dakota Community Foundation, 471
Northern Trust Company Charitable Trust, 181
Northwestern National Insurance Foundation, 667

Northwestern National Life Foundation, 350
Norton Company Foundation, 272
Norton Foundation, Inc., 236
Noyes, Jr. (Nicholas H.) Memorial Fdn., 212
Nuhn (Jane W.) Charitable Trust, 439

O

O'Brien (Alice M.) Foundation, 351
O'Connor (Kathryn) Foundation, 620
O'Fallon (Martin J. and Mary Anne)Trust, 81
O'Neil (Casey Albert T.) Foundation, 352
Ordean Foundation, 353
Oregon Community Foundation, 524
Owsley (Alvin and Lucy) Foundation, 621
Oxford Industries Foundation, Inc., 136

P

Palisades Educational Foundation, Inc., 440
Parker (Albert N.) Charitable Trust, 137
Parker, Jr. (William A.) Foundation, 138
Payne (Frank E.) and Seba B. Payne Fdn., 182
Peninsula Community Foundation, 54
Perpetual Trust for Charitable Giving, 273
PET Incorporated Community Support Fdn., 371
Pew Charitable Trusts, 547
Pfizer Foundation, Inc., 441
PHH Foundation, Inc., 253
Philadelphia Foundation, 548
Phillips (L.E.) Family Foundation, Inc., 668
Phillips Petroleum Foundation, Inc., 518
Pick, Jr. (Albert) Fund, 183
Plankenhorn (Harry) Foundation, Inc., 549
Plough Foundation, 582
Plum Foundation, 55
Plumsock Fund, 213
PNC Bank Foundation, 550
Polaroid Foundation, Inc., 274
Polk Bros. Foundation, Inc., 184
Pott (Herman T. and Phenie R.) Foundation, 372
Potter (Justin and Valere) Foundation, 583
Powell Family Foundation, 231
PPG Industries Foundation, 551
Prentiss (Elisabeth Severance) Foundation, 500
Price (Louis and Harold) Foundation, Inc., 442
Proctor (Mortimer R.) Trust, 634
Prospect Hill Foundation, Inc., 443

Providence Journal Charitable Foundation, 567
Public Welfare Foundation, Inc., 102
Puerto Rico Community Foundation, 565
Pulitzer Publishing Company Foundation, 373

R

Raker (M.E.) Foundation, 214
Rapoport (Paul) Foundation, Inc., 444
Raskob Foundation for Catholic Activities, 94
Ratshesky (A.C.) Foundation, 275
Ray Foundation, 153
Reed Foundation, 237
Reeves Foundation, 501
Reinberger Foundation, 502
Reinhold (Paul E. & Klare N.) Foundation, 116
Relations Foundation, 185
Reynolds (Kate B.) Charitable Trust, 467
Reynolds (Z. Smith) Foundation, Inc., 468
Rhode Island Foundation/Rhode Island Community Foundation, 568
Richardson (Sid W.) Foundation, 622
Richland County Fdn. of Mansfield, Ohio, 503
Rinker, Sr. (M.E.) Foundation, Inc., 117
Ritter (Gerald and May Ellen) Memorial Fund, 445
RJR Nabisco Foundation, 103
Robinson (E.O.) Mountain Fund, 238
Rockford Community Trust, 186
Rockwell Foundation, 552
Rockwell Fund, Inc., 623
Rodman Foundation, 354
Rubinstein (Helena) Foundation, Inc., 446
Russell (Sophie) Testamentary Trust, 147

S

Sage Foundation, 313
Salmen Family Foundation, 244
San Antonio Area Foundation, 624
San Francisco Foundation, 56
Sandy (George H.) Foundation, 57
Sara Lee Foundation, 187
Scaife Family Foundation, 553
Scaife (Sarah) Foundation, Inc., 554
Schering-Plough Foundation, Inc., 397
Scherman Foundation, Inc., 447
Schrafft (William E.) and Bertha E. Schrafft Charitable Trust, 276
Schramm Foundation, 82
Schultz Foundation, 398
Schumann (Florence and John) Foundation, 399
Schumann Fund for New Jersey, Inc., 400
Schwartz (Arnold A.) Foundation, 401
Seabrook (Harold S.) Charitable Trust, 16
Sears-Swetland Foundation, 504
Sequoia Foundation, 652
Shaw (Gardiner Howland) Foundation, 277
Sherwin-Williams Foundation, 505
Shore Fund, 555
Shubert Foundation, Inc., 448
Siebert Lutheran Foundation, Inc., 669
Simmons Foundation, Inc., 247
Simmons (Harold) Foundation, 625
Sister Fund, 449
Skillman Foundation, 314
Skinner Foundation, 653
Slawik (Harold J. and Marie O'Brien) Fdn., 355
Slusher (Roy W.) Charitable Foundation, 374
Smith (Ethel Sergeant Clark) Memorial Fund, 556
Smith (Hoxie Harrison) Foundation, 557
Smith (W.W.) Charitable Trust, 558
Smith (Kelvin and Eleanor) Foundation, 506
Smith, Jr. (M.W.) Foundation, 5
Smith (Stanley) Horticultural Trust, 58
SNC Foundation, Inc., 670
Snyder (Valentine Perry) Fund, 450
Sonat Foundation, Inc., 6
Sony Corporation of America Foundation, 451
Soule (Edward L. & Addie M.) Foundation, 59
South Atlantic Foundation, Inc., 139
South Dakota Community Foundation, 576
Spartanburg County Foundation, 573
Speas (John W. and Effie E.) Memorial Trust, 375
Speas (Victor E.) Foundation, 376
Sprague (Seth) Educational and Charitable Foundation, 452
Springs Foundation, 574
SPS Foundation, 559
Square D Foundation, 188
St. Croix Foundation, 356
St. Louis Community Foundation, 377
Stackner Family Foundation, Inc., 671
Stamps (James L.) Foundation, Inc., 60
State Street Foundation, 278
Stein (Jules and Doris) Foundation, 61
Stern (Alex) Family Foundation, 472

149

Stern (Irvin) Foundation, 189
Stevens (Abbot and Dorothy) Foundation, 279
Stevens (Nathaniel and Elizabeth P.) Fdn., 280
Stewart (Alexander and Margaret) Trust u/w of the late Helen S. Devore, 104
Stocker Foundation, 507
Stone (H. Chase) Trust, 83
Stott (Louis L.) Foundation, 560
Straus (Aaron) and Lillie Straus Fdn., 254
Stride Rite Charitable Foundation, Inc., 281
Stuart Foundation, 387
Stuart (Elbridge & Mary) Foundation, 62
Stuart Foundations, 63
Stulsaft (Morris) Foundation, 64
Stupp (Norman J.) Foundation, 378
Sunstrand Corporation Foundation, 190
Swalm Foundation, 626
Swisher Foundation, Inc., 215

T

Tait (Frank M.) Foundation, 508
Taubman (A. Alfred) Foundation, 315
Taubman Charitable Foundation, 316
Tektronix Foundation, 525
Thomas (Theresa A.) Memorial Foundation, 639
Thorpe (James R.) Foundation, 357
Times Mirror Foundation, 65
Titus (C.W.) Foundation, 519
Tomlinson Family Foundation, Inc., 402
Tonkin (Tom and Helen) Foundation, 674
Tonya Memorial Foundation, 584
Tozer Foundation, Inc., 358
Transamerica Foundation, 66
Travelers Companies Foundation, 90
Treakle (J. Edwin) Foundation, Inc., 640
Trexler (Harry C.) Trust, 561
Trident Community Foundation, 575
Trull Foundation, 627
TRW Foundation, 509
Tucker (Rose E.) Charitable Trust, 526
Turner (Courtney S.) Charitable Trust, 379
Turrell Fund, 403

U

Union Electric Company Charitable Trust, 380
United States Sugar Corporation Charitable Trust, 118
United States Trust Company of New York Foundation, 453
Universal Leaf Foundation, 641
US WEST Foundation, 84
USX Foundation, Inc., 562

V

Valley Foundation, 67
van Ameringen Foundation, Inc., 454
Vaughan (Rachael & Ben) Foundation, 628
Vidinha (A. & E.) Charitable Trust, 148

W

W.W.W. Foundation, 68
Wachovia Foundation Inc., 469
Wahlstrom Foundation, Inc., 119
Walsh (Blanche M.) Charity Trust, 282
Ward (A. Montgomery) Foundation, 191
Wardlaw (Gertrude and William C.) Fund, 140
Warner-Lambert Charitable Foundation, 404
Warren Memorial Foundation, 248
Washington Forrest Foundation, 642
Weatherwax Foundation, 317
Webb Foundation, 381
Webb (Del E.) Foundation, 12
Webster (Edwin S.) Foundation, 283
Wehle (Louis A.) Foundation, 455
Weintraub (Joseph) Family Foundation, 120
Weir Foundation Trust, 255
Westfield Foundation, 405
Whirlpool Foundation, 318
White Consolidated Industries Foundation, 510
White (Thomas H.) Foundation, 511
White (W.P. and H.B.) Foundation, 192
Whittier (L.K.) Foundation, 69
Wickes (Harvey Randall) Foundation, 319
Wickson-Link Memorial Foundation, 320
Wieboldt Foundation, 193
Wiggins (J. J.) Memorial Trust, 121
Wilkens (Ralph) Foundation, 456
Wilson (Lula C.) Trust, 321
Wilson (Marie C. and Joseph C.) Foundation, 457
Wilson (Matilda R.) Fund, 322
Wisconsin Power and Light Foundation, Inc., 672
Wisconsin Public Service Foundation, Inc., 673
Wolfe Associates Inc., 512

Woods Charitable Fund, Inc., 194
Woods-Greer Foundation, 585
World Heritage Foundation, 323
Wortham Foundation, 629
Wurts (Henrietta Tower) Memorial, 563
Wyomissing Foundation, Inc., 564

Y

Yellow Corporate Foundation, 232

Z

Zarrow (Anne and Henry) Foundation, 520
Zigler (Fred B. and Ruth B.) Foundation, 245

Index to Foundations

(Subject Index)

Citations are by entry number

AIDS—8, 19, 32, 41, 48, 51, 55, 66, 87, 95, 115, 136, 159, 163, 182, 201, 274, 323, 357, 362, 365, 376, 408, 414, 416, 417, 422, 425, 433, 435, 436, 438, 444, 447, 449, 460, 467, 481, 488, 534, 535, 558, 565, 568, 613, 627, 628, 635, 648, 666

ANIMAL WELFARE—10, 20, 40, 44, 63, 68, 72, 83, 93, 116, 131, 141, 143, 147, 160, 166, 173, 176, 182, 209, 229, 262, 302, 309, 315, 317, 339, 349, 354, 367, 370, 391, 411, 424, 443, 476, 515, 595, 600, 604, 624, 630, 641, 643, 652

COMMUNITY DEVELOPMENT—1, 3, 8, 10, 14, 21, 23, 27, 30, 31, 35, 36, 39, 40, 41, 43, 47, 48, 51, 56, 71, 74, 75, 78, 80, 84, 86, 87, 95, 96, 100, 101, 108, 116, 118, 121, 123, 124, 127, 129, 136, 141, 145, 146, 149, 150, 157, 158, 168, 169, 171, 174, 176, 177, 181, 183, 188, 189, 192, 193, 194, 197, 201, 206, 208, 210, 211, 217, 221, 229, 230, 231, 234, 239, 243, 246, 252, 253, 256, 257, 258, 265, 268, 269, 270, 271, 274, 275, 276, 277, 278, 279, 283, 284, 289, 293, 294, 298, 299, 300, 301, 303, 304, 307, 309, 312, 318, 319, 321, 324, 325, 326, 327, 331, 335, 336, 337, 339, 341, 345, 346, 347, 348, 355, 358, 359, 360, 362, 363, 366, 367, 371, 377, 380, 388, 393, 394, 399, 404, 405, 406, 409, 410, 411, 413, 416, 420, 432, 444, 450, 451, 453, 455, 468, 472, 481, 483, 485, 488, 489, 490, 493, 497, 513, 514, 515, 524, 525, 526, 527, 528, 533, 534, 538, 543, 545, 547, 550, 556, 559, 563, 575, 577, 579, 585, 600, 608, 616, 625, 627, 629, 660

CULTURAL ORGANIZATIONS—1, 2, 3, 5, 6, 8, 9, 10, 11, 14, 16, 18, 23, 25, 26, 27, 28, 29, 30, 31, 32, 36, 37, 38, 39, 40, 41, 47, 48, 49, 50, 51, 52, 53, 54, 58, 60, 61, 62, 65, 66, 67, 68, 69, 71, 72, 74, 75, 78, 83, 85, 87, 88, 89, 90, 91, 92, 93, 95, 96, 100, 105, 108, 111, 112, 113, 114, 119, 120, 122, 123, 124, 126, 127, 129, 130, 131, 133, 135, 136, 137, 138, 139, 141, 142, 143, 144, 145, 146, 149, 151, 155, 156, 157, 161, 162, 163, 170, 171, 172, 176, 177, 178, 179, 180, 181, 182, 183, 184, 186, 187, 190, 194, 196, 197, 198, 199, 201, 202, 204, 206, 207, 209, 210, 211, 212, 213, 215, 216, 217, 218, 221, 222, 224, 226, 232, 233, 235, 236, 240, 243, 250, 251, 252, 253, 254, 255, 256, 257, 258, 265, 266, 267, 270, 271, 272, 274, 275, 276, 278, 279, 280, 281, 283, 287, 288, 289, 290, 291, 292, 294, 296, 297, 299, 300, 301, 302, 303, 304, 305, 306, 308, 309, 310, 311, 312, 313, 314, 315, 316, 317, 318, 319, 320, 321, 322, 323, 324, 325, 328, 330, 331, 332, 333, 334, 335, 336, 338, 339, 340, 342, 343, 344, 345, 346, 347, 348, 349, 350, 351, 354, 356, 357, 358, 359, 362, 363, 364, 366, 367, 371, 373, 377, 379, 380, 382, 383, 384, 385, 386, 388, 389, 391, 393, 394, 395, 397, 398, 402, 406, 408, 410, 411, 416, 417, 418, 420, 421, 423, 424, 425, 426, 428, 429, 431, 432, 433, 436, 438, 441, 442, 443, 445, 447, 448, 451, 452, 453, 455, 456, 457, 458, 459, 460, 461, 468, 469, 470, 471, 473, 474, 477, 478, 479, 481, 482, 483, 485, 486, 487, 488, 489, 490, 491, 492, 493, 494, 495, 496, 498, 499, 501, 502, 504, 505, 506, 507, 508, 509, 510, 512, 515, 516, 517, 518, 519, 520, 522, 523, 524, 526, 528, 530, 531, 532, 533, 534, 536, 539, 540, 542, 543, 544, 547, 548, 550, 551, 552, 556, 559, 561, 562, 564, 565, 566, 567, 569, 571, 572, 573, 576, 577, 579, 581, 582, 583, 585, 586, 587, 588, 589, 592, 593, 594, 603, 605, 610, 612, 613, 614, 615, 616, 618, 620, 622, 623, 625, 628, 629, 632, 634, 637, 638, 641, 642, 646, 647, 648, 649, 650, 652, 653, 654, 655, 656, 657, 659, 660, 661, 662, 663, 664, 665, 667, 668, 670, 672, 673

DISABLED—1, 2, 4, 5, 6, 8, 9, 10, 12, 13, 19, 20, 23, 24, 26, 27, 31, 33, 34, 35, 36, 38, 39, 40, 44, 45, 46, 47, 49, 51, 52, 54, 57, 59, 63, 71, 74, 79, 82, 84, 87, 89, 92, 95, 97, 99, 104, 105, 106, 109, 110, 111, 113, 115, 119, 120, 122, 123, 126, 127, 128, 139, 141, 142, 145, 146, 147, 148, 149, 151, 153, 154, 155, 156, 158, 159, 160, 161, 162, 163, 164, 165, 166, 168, 172, 173, 174, 175, 178, 180, 181, 182, 187, 188, 189, 190, 194, 195, 196, 197, 199, 200, 201, 206, 210, 212, 215, 217, 218, 219, 220, 221, 224, 226, 228, 229, 234, 236, 237, 238, 239, 241, 243, 245, 246, 249, 250, 251, 252, 253, 254, 258, 260, 261, 263, 264, 270, 273, 274, 284, 291, 293, 294, 296, 298, 302, 303, 304, 306, 309, 312, 313, 314, 315, 318, 320, 321, 322, 324, 327, 334, 335, 336, 337, 343, 344, 345, 347, 348, 350, 352, 353, 357, 358, 367, 368, 369, 370, 372, 375, 376, 377, 380, 381, 392, 394, 401, 402, 403, 405, 406, 408, 409, 410, 411, 414, 424, 427, 431, 433, 436, 437, 442, 446, 460, 470, 472, 473, 476, 478, 481, 491, 494, 496, 499, 500, 509, 515, 519, 520, 523, 524, 526, 529, 547, 548, 549, 552, 553, 556, 557, 558, 561, 562, 566, 568, 571, 572, 578, 586, 592, 600, 605, 606, 609, 613, 616, 618, 621, 624, 627, 628, 631, 635, 637, 648, 649, 651, 653, 654, 659, 660, 661, 665, 666, 667, 671, 674

EDUCATION (other than higher education)—1, 3, 4, 14, 37, 38, 44, 51, 52, 55, 58, 59, 63, 68, 69, 76, 79, 81, 83, 84, 87, 88, 93, 96, 103, 117, 120, 121, 124, 126, 129, 136, 137, 138, 141, 142, 151, 153, 163, 164, 174, 182, 190, 196, 198, 200, 201, 205, 214, 222, 223, 237, 242, 249, 272, 273, 276, 287, 291, 296, 297, 306, 314, 317, 320, 329, 334, 335, 336, 341, 343, 369, 389, 402, 417, 426, 450, 461, 465, 476, 481, 484, 489, 495, 508, 514, 526, 530, 536, 539, 569, 571, 580, 581, 584, 587, 633, 646, 663, 667, 669

ELDERLY—9, 10, 13, 18, 19, 20, 24, 26, 33, 34, 35, 40, 45, 46, 47, 49, 50, 52, 56, 70, 71, 77, 79, 90, 91, 95, 97, 102, 109, 119, 127, 131, 143, 145, 150, 160, 163, 168, 189, 196, 206, 210, 219, 220, 234, 244, 245, 255, 260, 263, 264, 268, 291, 299, 302, 333, 346, 357, 367, 372, 375, 376, 377, 394, 395, 402, 409, 420, 422, 427, 441, 443, 450, 463, 467, 471, 478, 513, 523, 529, 556, 557, 558, 562, 565, 568, 586, 651, 665, 670

ENVIRONMENT—5, 7, 9, 18, 24, 25, 29, 35, 36, 41, 44, 50, 54, 55, 56, 72, 80, 92, 102, 115, 118, 129, 142, 143, 145, 155, 158, 160, 166, 170, 174, 176, 179, 183, 193, 196, 198, 234, 235, 236, 252, 259, 262, 265, 269, 270, 271, 279, 280, 324, 326, 328, 354, 377, 399, 407, 414, 418, 436, 443, 447, 458, 459, 468, 476, 477, 487, 488, 489, 491, 495, 496, 522, 529, 530, 534, 540, 545, 547, 552, 555, 560, 564, 572, 579, 613, 618, 628, 644, 646, 652, 661, 663

HEALTH ORGANIZATIONS—1, 4, 6, 9, 12, 14, 20, 23, 26, 27, 30, 35, 45, 46, 47, 48, 49, 51, 53, 54, 55, 56, 59, 61, 63, 68, 70, 71, 72, 73, 74, 75, 76, 78, 79, 85, 86, 89, 92, 94, 95, 96, 101, 104, 106, 108, 109, 110, 113, 116, 117, 120, 123, 127, 128, 130, 135, 136, 137, 139, 140, 141, 142, 143, 144, 145, 146, 147, 148, 151, 153, 155, 156, 158, 162, 163, 164, 166, 168, 173, 175, 177, 178, 179, 182, 183, 188, 192, 195, 196, 201, 205, 208, 209, 210, 213, 215, 218, 219, 220, 222, 224, 225, 227, 228, 229, 230, 232, 238, 239, 245, 248, 250, 251, 253, 255, 256, 257, 258, 260, 261, 264, 266, 273, 274, 278, 280, 284, 287, 289, 291, 293, 297, 298, 299, 302, 304, 308, 312, 313, 315, 317, 320, 323, 327, 339, 344, 346, 348, 349, 350, 352, 353, 356, 357, 362, 367, 369, 370, 376, 378, 381, 382, 383, 390, 392, 394, 395, 397, 398, 406, 408, 412, 413, 414, 415, 416, 417, 422, 423, 425, 427, 430, 431, 433, 435, 437, 441, 442, 443, 447, 450, 451, 452, 453, 454, 456, 457, 459, 461, 465, 467, 469, 470, 471, 476, 478, 479, 483, 485, 486, 489, 491, 493, 494, 495, 498, 500, 503, 504, 505, 509, 512, 513, 514, 515, 516, 519, 520, 522, 523, 524, 525, 526, 529, 530, 532, 533, 535, 540, 541, 542, 543, 544, 548, 549, 550, 551, 552, 553, 556, 559, 560, 561, 562, 563, 564, 565, 566, 568, 569, 571, 578, 580, 586, 587, 589, 590, 591, 593, 595, 596, 597, 598, 599, 600, 602, 605, 608, 610, 611, 613, 618, 619, 620, 621, 623, 624, 626, 627, 628, 630, 631, 632, 633, 635, 639, 640, 641, 642, 648, 651, 653, 654, 660, 661, 662, 663, 664, 665, 666, 667, 670, 671, 672, 673, 674

HIGHER EDUCATION—1, 2, 4, 17, 22, 28, 34, 41, 51, 52, 55, 63, 84, 85, 87, 89, 96, 97, 103, 110, 112, 117, 118, 119, 120, 123, 124, 126, 127, 129, 131, 132, 133, 136, 138, 155, 164, 171, 174, 190, 196, 198, 201, 202, 205, 207, 209, 216, 217, 226, 237, 238, 242, 252, 272, 276, 284, 285, 288, 291, 296, 297, 300, 301, 304, 314, 315, 316, 319, 320, 323, 329, 335, 336, 341, 342, 343, 349, 354, 361, 369, 379, 386, 390, 391, 392, 410, 426, 450, 461, 463, 465, 466, 468, 473, 475, 489, 533, 544, 555, 580, 587, 619, 620, 631, 636, 643, 645, 648, 655, 667, 669, 670

HOSPITALS—1, 2, 12, 20, 21, 33, 46, 50, 53, 59, 61, 62, 63, 68, 79, 82, 89, 94, 100, 108, 110, 111, 117, 120, 122, 126, 130, 131, 135, 136, 137, 141, 154, 155, 156, 168, 175, 177, 180, 182, 188, 191, 192, 195, 208, 212, 215, 217, 225, 229, 238, 239, 242, 255, 257, 261, 273, 276, 291, 294, 296, 302, 303, 308, 310, 312, 313, 320, 323, 326, 334, 340, 349, 350, 354, 356, 359, 363, 365, 369, 370, 378, 380, 381, 389, 395, 397, 404, 413, 417, 419, 420, 435, 451, 454, 459, 463, 474, 489, 490, 495, 500, 503, 509, 512, 513, 514, 519, 529, 531, 535, 538, 548, 555, 557, 566, 574, 590, 597, 598, 602, 605, 606, 617, 619, 620, 630, 635, 648, 658, 662, 667, 670

MINORITIES—1, 17, 18, 19, 23, 26, 39, 41, 46, 54, 57, 74, 80, 84, 102, 103, 111, 112, 114, 127, 159, 171, 174, 178, 181, 187, 189, 190, 193, 196, 197, 198, 207, 209, 210, 211, 212, 263, 270, 275, 276, 278, 283, 300, 302, 315, 316, 327, 336, 338, 343, 347, 361, 373, 408, 410, 412, 413, 414, 417, 424, 429, 436, 437, 438, 441, 449, 461, 468, 481, 488, 509, 527, 558, 618, 627, 636, 671

RELIGIOUS ORGANIZATIONS—3, 4, 14, 20, 28, 44, 47, 50, 55, 59, 60, 68, 72, 82, 85, 88, 93, 94, 96, 106, 112, 117, 120, 123, 126, 129, 131, 132, 134, 136, 137, 138, 141, 142, 144, 175, 182, 185, 189, 196, 197, 198, 203, 204, 209, 212, 222, 223, 225, 226, 241, 254, 255, 282, 293, 294, 295, 306, 315, 317, 320, 349, 354, 355, 356, 364, 365, 374, 385, 386, 387, 389, 390, 396, 402, 422, 428, 430, 434, 442, 443, 445, 461, 495, 515, 541, 569, 571, 578, 580, 585, 591, 592, 596, 607, 616, 620, 623, 626, 627, 633, 635, 640, 668, 669

SOCIAL WELFARE—1, 2, 4, 6, 8, 9, 10, 11, 12, 15, 16, 18, 19, 20, 21, 22, 23, 24, 25, 26, 27, 30, 31, 34, 36, 37, 39, 40, 41, 42, 44, 46, 47, 49, 50, 51, 52, 54, 59, 61, 62, 63, 64, 66, 68, 69, 70, 71, 72, 73, 74, 75, 76, 77, 80, 82, 84, 86, 87, 88, 89, 91, 92, 94, 97, 99, 101, 102, 105, 106, 109, 110, 112, 113, 115, 116, 117, 118, 120, 122, 125, 126, 127, 128, 129, 130, 136, 137, 139, 140, 141, 142, 143, 144, 145, 146, 147, 149, 151, 155, 156, 157, 159, 163, 164, 165, 166, 167, 168, 169, 170, 171, 172, 178, 179, 180, 181, 182, 183, 184, 185, 186, 187, 189, 191, 192, 194, 196, 197, 199, 201, 202, 205, 207, 208, 209, 215, 216, 217, 218, 219, 220, 222, 224, 225, 227, 229, 230, 232, 234, 235, 236, 239, 241, 242, 244, 246, 247, 248, 249, 250, 251, 252, 253, 254, 255, 256, 257, 259, 261, 262, 263, 264, 265, 268, 270, 272, 274, 275, 277, 278, 279, 280, 281, 282, 284, 285, 288, 289, 290, 291, 293, 294, 295, 296, 297, 298, 299, 300, 302, 303, 304, 305, 306, 307, 309, 310, 311, 314, 315, 317, 318, 320, 321, 322, 323, 324, 325, 327, 328, 330, 331, 332, 333, 334, 335, 337, 340, 341, 343, 344, 345, 346, 347, 349, 350, 351, 352, 353, 354, 355, 356, 357, 358, 359, 362, 363, 364, 365, 366, 367, 368, 370, 371, 372, 373, 374, 375, 377, 378, 380, 381, 382, 386, 388, 390, 391, 392, 393, 398, 400, 401, 402, 403, 404, 405, 406, 409, 410, 411, 412, 413, 414, 415, 416, 417, 420, 421, 422, 423, 424, 425, 428, 429, 430, 431, 432, 433, 434, 435, 436, 437, 438, 440, 441, 442, 444, 445, 446, 447, 449, 450, 452, 454, 455, 456, 457, 458, 459, 460, 461, 462, 463, 464, 466, 467, 468, 469, 470, 471, 472, 474, 476, 477, 479, 481, 483, 484, 485, 486, 487, 488, 489, 494, 496, 498, 499, 500, 502, 503, 504, 505, 507, 509, 510, 511, 512, 513, 514, 515, 517, 518, 519, 520, 522, 524, 525, 526, 527, 528, 529, 530, 531, 533, 535, 537, 538, 540, 541, 542, 543, 544, 545, 546, 547, 548, 549, 550, 551, 552, 553, 555, 556, 557, 558, 560, 561, 562, 563, 564, 566, 568, 569, 570, 571, 572, 575, 576, 577, 578, 581, 582, 583, 586, 587, 588, 589, 591, 592, 593, 594, 595, 596, 598, 599, 600, 601, 602, 603, 604, 605, 607, 608, 609, 610, 611, 612, 613, 614, 615, 616, 618, 621, 622, 623, 624, 625, 626, 627, 628, 629, 631, 632, 634, 635, 636, 637, 638, 640, 641, 642, 647, 648, 649, 650, 651, 652, 653, 654, 656, 657, 658, 659, 661, 664, 665, 666, 667, 668, 669, 670, 671, 672, 673, 674

WOMEN—3, 14, 23, 26, 33, 37, 51, 62, 69, 81, 94, 96, 98, 131, 163, 164, 168, 171, 176, 178, 181, 187, 216, 226, 239, 249, 252, 269, 274, 275, 277, 284, 321, 327, 350, 353, 358, 402, 408, 417, 427, 441, 446, 449, 456, 458, 468, 476, 488, 511, 522, 523, 526, 537, 556, 558, 563, 564, 595, 601, 618, 623, 628, 632, 633, 636, 648, 670

YOUTH ORGANIZATIONS—1, 3, 4, 5, 8, 9, 11, 12, 14, 15, 16, 17, 18, 19, 20, 21, 22, 23, 24, 26, 27, 29, 32, 33, 35, 36, 37, 38, 39, 40, 41, 42, 44, 45, 46, 47, 50, 51, 52, 53, 54, 55, 57, 59, 60, 62, 63, 64, 65, 66, 68, 69, 70, 71, 72, 73, 74, 77, 78, 79, 82, 84, 85, 86, 89, 90, 92, 94, 96, 97, 103, 107, 109, 112, 113, 114, 115, 116, 118, 120, 121, 123, 125, 127, 128, 129, 130, 133, 136, 137, 138, 140, 141, 142, 143, 144, 145, 146, 151, 153, 154, 155, 156, 157, 159, 161, 164, 165, 166, 168, 169, 170, 171, 172, 174, 175, 177, 178, 180, 181, 182, 187, 190, 191, 192, 194, 195, 196, 198, 200, 201, 203, 204, 205, 207, 208, 209, 211, 212, 214, 215, 216, 217, 219, 220, 221, 222, 223, 224, 226, 228, 229, 230, 231, 236, 237, 238, 239, 240, 241, 244, 245, 248, 249, 251, 252, 254, 255, 257, 258, 259, 261, 263, 264, 266, 268, 269, 270, 272, 273, 274, 275, 276, 277, 278, 279, 281, 283, 284, 288, 289, 290, 291, 292, 293, 294, 296, 297, 298, 301, 302, 304, 305, 306, 307, 308, 309, 311, 313, 314, 315, 317, 319, 320, 321, 322, 323, 325, 326, 327, 328, 330, 331, 332, 334, 336, 337, 338, 341, 342, 343, 344, 345, 348, 349, 350, 352, 353, 354, 355, 356, 357, 358, 360, 363, 364, 365, 367, 368, 369, 370, 371, 372, 373, 375, 376, 378, 381, 382, 385, 386, 387, 392, 394, 400, 401, 403, 404, 405, 406, 408, 409, 411, 412, 413, 414, 416, 419, 420, 421, 422, 423, 427, 430, 432, 434, 435, 441, 442, 445, 446, 449, 450, 451, 452, 454, 456, 457, 458, 459, 460, 461, 463, 464, 467, 468, 469, 470, 471, 472, 473, 476, 478, 481, 483, 484, 487, 488, 489, 493, 494, 495, 496, 498, 503, 504, 507, 508, 509, 512, 514, 515, 518, 521, 524, 527, 528, 529, 533, 537, 538, 540, 545, 546, 547, 548, 549, 550, 551, 555, 557, 558, 559, 561, 562, 563, 564, 567, 569, 571, 578, 579, 580, 581, 586, 588, 589, 592, 593, 595, 596, 598, 599, 601, 602, 604, 606, 607, 608, 609, 611, 615, 616, 617, 618, 625, 628, 629, 630, 631, 632, 635, 637, 643, 646, 648, 649, 652, 653, 654, 656, 658, 659, 663, 665, 666, 667, 670, 671, 674

Comments

Thank you for purchasing the Second Edition of the *Directory of Operating Grants*. We welcome your comments (positive and negative). Please list funding sources that should be included in this *Directory*.

Thank you for your response.

Comments:

Name_____Title_____

Organization _____

Address _____

City_____State_____Zip_____

Please send comments to: Editor
Research Grant Guides, Inc.
P.O. Box 1214
Loxahatchee, FL 33470